CHARLES VANCE

Learn C#

Powered by chatGPT

First edition

This book was professionally typeset on Reedsy.
Find out more at reedsy.com

Contents

1

Introduction to C#

C# (pronounced "see sharp") is a modern, multi-paradigm programming language developed by Microsoft as part of the .NET initiative. C# is designed to be simple, powerful, and type-safe, making it a popular choice for building a wide range of applications, including web and desktop applications, video games, mobile apps, and cloud services.

C# was first released in 2000 and has since evolved through multiple versions, with the latest being C# 10, which was released in 2021. C# is a statically typed language that supports object-oriented programming, functional programming, and asynchronous programming. It is strongly influenced by C++, Java, and other programming languages.

C# is often used in conjunction with the .NET Framework or .NET Core, which provide a set of libraries and tools for building Windows applications and web services. C# is also commonly used with Xamarin, a cross-platform development tool that allows developers to write C# code and deploy it on iOS, Android, and other platforms.

Overall, C# is a versatile and powerful language that is well-suited for building a wide variety of applications, from small utilities to large enterprise systems.

Advantages

There are several advantages to using C# as a programming language:

1. Modern and Versatile Language: C# is a modern and versatile language that supports a wide range of programming paradigms, including object-oriented programming, functional programming, and asynchronous programming. This makes C# a powerful and flexible language that can be used to build a wide range of applications.

2. Type-Safe Language: C# is a type-safe language, which means that it provides strong type checking and ensures that code is free of type-related errors. This makes C# a reliable language that is less prone to runtime errors and crashes.

3. Easy to Learn and Use: C# is designed to be easy to learn and use, with a syntax that is similar to other popular programming languages such as C++ and Java. This makes it a great language for beginners who are just starting to learn programming, as well as experienced developers who are looking to pick up a new language.

4. Cross-Platform Support: C# is supported on multiple platforms, including Windows, macOS, and Linux, and can be used to build cross-platform applications. This makes C# a great choice for developers who want to build applications that can run on a variety of devices and operating systems.

5. Large Developer Community: C# has a large and active developer community, with a wealth of resources and tools available to developers. This makes it easy to get help and support when needed, as well as access to a wide range of libraries and frameworks that can be used to accelerate development.

6. Integration with .NET Framework and Tools: C# is closely integrated with the .NET Framework and other Microsoft tools, such as Visual Studio. This provides developers with a powerful set of tools and libraries that can be used to build and deploy applications quickly and efficiently.

Overall, C# is a powerful and versatile language that offers a range of benefits to developers. Its ease of use, strong type checking, cross-platform support, and large developer community make it an attractive choice for building a wide range of applications, from desktop and mobile apps to web services and video games.

Installing and Setting Up C#

Downloading and installing Visual Studio is a straightforward process. Here's a general outline of the steps:

1. Go to the Visual Studio website (**https://visualstudio.microsoft.com/ downloads/**) and select the version of Visual Studio you want to download. There are several editions to choose from, including Community, Professional, and Enterprise.
2. Once you've selected the edition you want, click the "Download" button to start the download process.
3. Depending on your internet speed, the download may take some time to complete. Once the download is finished, open the downloaded file to start the installation process.
4. The installation process will begin with a welcome screen. Click "Continue" to proceed.
5. Next, you'll be asked to choose the workloads you want to install. Workloads are groups of related features and tools that are required for specific types of development. Choose the workload that best fits your needs, or select "Individual Components" to choose specific features and tools to install.
6. Once you've selected your workloads or individual components, click "Install" to start the installation process.
7. The installation process may take some time, depending on the size of the selected workloads or components. Once the installation is finished, you'll be prompted to restart your computer.
8. After restarting your computer, you can launch Visual Studio and start

writing code.

Note that these steps are a general guide and may vary slightly depending on the version of Visual Studio you're installing and your specific operating system. It's always a good idea to follow the installation instructions provided by Microsoft to ensure a smooth installation process.

Create a new project

Creating a new project in Visual Studio is a simple process. Here's a general outline of the steps:

1. Open Visual Studio and select "Create a new project" from the welcome screen. If you've already opened Visual Studio, you can select "File" > "New" > "Project" from the top menu.
2. Next, you'll be prompted to choose the type of project you want to create. Visual Studio supports a wide range of project types, including console applications, Windows Forms applications, web applications, and more. Choose the project type that best fits your needs, or select "Blank Solution" to create a solution without any predefined project types.
3. After choosing the project type, you'll be prompted to choose a name and location for your project. Enter a name for your project and choose a location where you want to save the project files. You can also choose to create the project as part of a solution, which is a container that can hold multiple related projects.
4. Click "Create" to create the new project. Visual Studio will generate the necessary files and folders for your project and open the main project file in the editor.
5. At this point, you can start writing code for your project. Depending on the project type you chose, you may need to add references to additional libraries or frameworks in order to use certain features or functionality.

Note that these steps are a general guide and may vary slightly depending on the version of Visual Studio you're using and the specific project type you're creating. It's always a good idea to consult the Visual Studio documentation for more detailed instructions on creating new projects.

Hello World

Writing and running a "Hello, World!" program in C# is a great way to get started with the language. Here's a general outline of the steps:

1. Open Visual Studio and create a new console application project. To do this, select "Create a new project" from the welcome screen or select "File" > "New" > "Project" from the top menu, and then choose "Console Application" under the "C#" section.
2. Once the project is created, open the "Program.cs" file in the editor. This file contains the code for the main entry point of the console application.
3. In the "Main" method of the "Program" class, add the following line of code:

```
Console.WriteLine("Hello, World!");
```

This line of code will write the text "Hello, World!" to the console output.

1. Save the changes to the "Program.cs" file.
2. To run the program, select "Debug" > "Start Without Debugging" from the top menu or press the F5 key. This will compile and run the program.
3. The console output window will appear and display the text "Hello, World!". You've successfully written and run a simple C# program!

Note that these steps are a general guide and may vary slightly depending on the version of Visual Studio you're using. If you encounter any issues or errors, consult the Visual Studio documentation or online resources for troubleshooting tips.

Basic Syntax

Comments

Comments are a feature in C# that allow you to add notes and explanations to your code. Comments are ignored by the compiler and do not affect the execution of your code, but they can be very useful for helping others understand your code and for helping you remember what your code does. There are two types of comments in C#:

1. Single-line comments: These comments begin with two forward slashes (//) and continue until the end of the line. Single-line comments are typically used to explain specific lines of code or to provide brief notes.
2. Multi-line comments: These comments begin with /* and end with */. Multi-line comments can span multiple lines and are typically used for longer explanations or for temporarily disabling blocks of code.

Comments should be used sparingly and only when necessary. They should be clear, concise, and helpful to others who may be reading your code. It's important to remember to keep your comments up-to-date and relevant as your code changes over time.

Variables and data types (int, double, string, bool)

Variables are a fundamental concept in programming, and C# is no exception. A variable is a named storage location in memory that holds a value of a particular data type. In C#, you must declare a variable before you can use it.
Declaring a variable involves specifying its data type, followed by its name.

For example, to declare an integer variable named "num", you would write:

```
int num;
```

This tells the compiler that we want to allocate memory for an integer variable named "num". The value of "num" is initially undefined and can be set later in the code.

Initializing a variable involves assigning a value to the variable at the time of declaration. For example, to declare and initialize an integer variable named "num" with the value of 10, you would write:

```
int num = 10;
```

Variables can be used throughout your code to store and manipulate data. They can be used in expressions and can be updated or reassigned at any point in the program.

It's important to choose appropriate variable names that are descriptive and meaningful. For example, if you're using a variable to store the user's age, you might name it "userAge" instead of just "age". This makes the code more readable and easier to understand.

In summary, variables are a basic building block of any programming language, including C#. By declaring and initializing variables, you can store and manipulate data throughout your program.

Declaring and Initializing variables

Declaring and initializing variables is a fundamental concept in C# programming. Here's an overview of how to declare and initialize variables in C#:

To declare a variable in C#, you need to specify the data type of the variable followed by the variable name. For example, to declare a variable named "myVar" of type int, you would write:

```
12
13    int myVar;
14
15
```

Variables can also be declared and initialized at the same time. For example:

```
15
16    int myVar = 10;
17
18
```

In addition, you can declare multiple variables of the same type in a single line, separated by commas. For example:

```
19
20    int num1, num2, num3;
21
```

Initializing Variables:

- Initializing a variable means assigning a value to it. You can initialize a variable when you declare it, or at a later point in the program.
- To initialize a variable at declaration, you use the assignment operator (=) followed by the value. For example:

```
22
23    int myVar = 10;
24
```

To initialize a variable later in the program, you use the assignment operator (=) followed by the value. For example:

```
25
26    myVar = 20;
27
28
```

It's important to choose appropriate variable names that are descriptive and meaningful. Variable names should begin with a letter or underscore, and can include letters, numbers, and underscores. Variable names are case-sensitive in C#.

Data types in C#

Numeric

Numeric data types are a fundamental concept in C# programming. Here's an overview of the most commonly used numeric data types in C#:

1. int - the "int" data type is used to represent integer values. It is a 32-bit signed integer data type, which means it can represent values between -2,147,483,648 and 2,147,483,647.
2. double - the "double" data type is used to represent decimal values. It is a 64-bit floating-point data type, which means it can represent values with greater precision and a larger range than the "float" data type.
3. float - the "float" data type is also used to represent decimal values. It is a 32-bit floating-point data type, which means it can represent values with less precision and a smaller range than the "double" data type.
4. decimal - the "decimal" data type is used to represent decimal values with a high degree of precision. It is a 128-bit data type, which means it can represent values with up to 28-29 significant digits.

Here's an example of declaring and initializing variables of these numeric data types:

```
29
30      int myInt = 10;
31      double myDouble = 3.14;
32      float myFloat = 1.23f;
33      decimal myDecimal = 123.456m;
34
```

It's important to choose the appropriate data type for the task at hand, depending on the precision and range required. Using a data type with too little precision or too small a range can result in data loss or inaccurate calculations. Additionally, using a data type with too much precision can result in slower performance and increased memory usage.

Text

The "string" data type is used to represent text in C# programming. A string is a sequence of characters that can include letters, digits, and special characters. Here's an overview of how to declare and initialize variables of type string:
  Declaring and Initializing a String:

- To declare a string variable, you use the "string" keyword followed by the variable name. For example:

```
35
36      string myString;
37
```

- To initialize a string variable, you use the assignment operator (=) followed by the string value. For example:

```
39
40      myString = "Hello, World!";
41
42
```

- You can also declare and initialize a string variable in a single line. For example:

```
43
44    string myString = "Hello, World!";
45
46
```

String Methods:

- C# provides many built-in string methods that allow you to manipulate strings. For example, the "Length" method returns the length of the string, and the "Substring" method returns a substring of the original string. Here's an example:

```
47
48    string myString = "Hello, World!";
49    int length = myString.Length; // length = 13
50    string substring = myString.Substring(0, 5); // substring = "Hello"
51
52
```

String Concatenation:

- You can concatenate strings using the "+" operator or the "string.Concat" method. Here's an example:

```
53
54    string firstName = "John";
55    string lastName = "Doe";
56    string fullName = firstName + " " + lastName; // fullName = "John Doe"
57    string fullName2 = string.Concat(firstName, " ", lastName); // fullName2 =
58                                                                 //"John Doe"
59
```

String Formatting:

- C# also provides string formatting options that allow you to format string values. For example, the "ToString" method can be used to convert numeric values to strings with a specified format. Here's an example:

```
61
62   int num = 123;
63   string numString = num.ToString("D6"); // numString = "000123"
64
65
```

Boolean data type (bool)

The "bool" data type is used to represent Boolean values in C# programming. A Boolean value can be either true or false, and is often used in conditional statements and loops. Here's an overview of how to declare and initialize variables of type bool:

Declaring and Initializing a Boolean:

- To declare a bool variable, you use the "bool" keyword followed by the variable name. For example:

```
65
66
67   bool myBool;
68
69
```

- To initialize a bool variable, you use the assignment operator (=) followed by the boolean value. For example:

```
69
70
71    myBool = true;
72
73
```

- You can also declare and initialize a bool variable in a single line. For example:

```
74
75    bool myBool = false;
76
77
```

Boolean Operators:

- C# provides several operators that can be used with Boolean values. For example, the "&&" operator represents logical AND, the "||" operator represents logical OR, and the "!" operator represents logical NOT. Here's an example:

```
79    bool a = true;
80    bool b = false;
81    bool c = a && b; // c = false
82    bool d = a || b; // d = true
83    bool e = !a; // e = false
84
```

Boolean Comparisons:

- You can also compare Boolean values using the "==" and "!=" operators. Here's an example:

```
86
87    bool a = true;
88    bool b = false;
89    bool c = (a == b); // c = false
90    bool d = (a != b); // d = true
91
92
```

Other data types (char, datetime)

In addition to the numeric, text, and Boolean data types, C# also provides several other data types that can be used to represent different types of values. Here's an overview of the two most commonly used additional data types in C#:

1. char - the "char" data type is used to represent a single character. In C#, characters are enclosed in single quotes (''). For example, to declare a char variable named "myChar" with the value 'A', you would write:

```
93
94    char myChar = 'A';
95
96
97
```

- Char data types can also be represented by their Unicode values. For example, to declare a char variable named "myChar" with the value '♣', you would write:

```
97
98    char myChar = '\u2663';
99
100
```

14

DateTime - the "DateTime" data type is used to represent dates and times. It includes properties such as Year, Month, Day, Hour, Minute, Second, and Millisecond. For example, to declare a DateTime variable named "myDateTime" with the current date and time, you would write:

```
101
102    DateTime myDateTime = DateTime.Now;
103
104
```

- DateTime values can also be initialized with a specific date and time using the DateTime constructor. For example:

```
104
105
106    DateTime myDateTime = new DateTime(2022, 5, 1, 10, 30, 0);
107
108
```

It's important to choose the appropriate data type for the task at hand, depending on the type of value being represented. Using the wrong data type can result in data loss or inaccurate calculations.

Type conversion and casting

In C#, you can convert one data type to another using type conversion. Type conversion is the process of converting a value from one data type to another data type. There are two types of type conversion in C#: implicit type conversion and explicit type conversion.

1. Implicit Type Conversion Implicit type conversion is a type of type conversion where the conversion is done automatically by the compiler. Implicit type conversion is allowed when there is no loss of information

during the conversion. For example, converting an int to a long is an implicit type conversion because a long can represent all the values of an int.

Here's an example of implicit type conversion:

```
109
110    int myInt = 10;
111    long myLong = myInt; // implicit type conversion from int to long
112
113
```

Explicit Type Conversion Explicit type conversion is a type of type conversion where the conversion is done by the programmer using a cast operator. Explicit type conversion is required when there is a possibility of loss of information during the conversion. For example, converting a double to an int requires explicit type conversion because the decimal portion of the double will be lost when converted to an int.

Here's an example of explicit type conversion:

```
114
115    double myDouble = 3.14;
116    int myInt = (int)myDouble; // explicit type conversion from double to int
117
118
```

It's important to use type conversion carefully to avoid data loss or inaccurate calculations. Implicit type conversion is generally safer than explicit type conversion because it is done automatically by the compiler, but it's important to be aware of the limitations of implicit type conversion.

Operators

Operators are symbols or keywords used to perform operations on one or more operands in C# programming. C# provides several arithmetic operators that can be used to perform mathematical calculations on numeric values.

Here's an overview of the most commonly used arithmetic operators in C#:

- Addition (+) - the addition operator is used to add two or more values together. For example:

```
119
120    int a = 5;
121    int b = 10;
122    int c = a + b; // c = 15
123
```

- Subtraction (-) - the subtraction operator is used to subtract one value from another. For example:

```
125
126    int a = 10;
127    int b = 5;
128    int c = a - b; // c = 5
129
```

- Multiplication (*) - the multiplication operator is used to multiply two or more values together. For example:

```
131
132    int a = 5;
133    int b = 10;
134    int c = a * b; // c = 50
135
```

- Division (/) - the division operator is used to divide one value by another. For example:

```
137
138      int a = 10;
139      int b = 5;
140      int c = a / b; // c = 2
141
```

Note that if both operands are integers, the result will be an integer, which means any remainder will be truncated. If you want to get a floating-point result, you need to use a floating-point data type for at least one of the operands.

- Modulus (%) - the modulus operator is used to get the remainder of a division operation. For example:

```
143
144      int a = 10;
145      int b = 3;
146      int c = a % b; // c = 1
147
148
```

These operators can be used in combination to perform more complex mathematical calculations.

Operators are symbols or keywords used to perform operations on one or more operands in C# programming. C# provides several arithmetic operators, including addition, subtraction, multiplication, division, and modulus. These operators can be used to perform mathematical calculations on numeric values.

Basic input/output using Console.WriteLine() and Console.ReadLine()

Input/output is a fundamental aspect of programming, as it allows the program to interact with the user. In C#, the Console class provides methods for input/output using the console window. Two of the most commonly used methods are Console.WriteLine() and Console.ReadLine().

Console.WriteLine() The Console.WriteLine() method is used to output text to the console window. It takes a string as an argument and prints it to the console, followed by a newline character. Here's an example:

```
149
150    Console.WriteLine("Hello, World!");
151
152
```

This code will output "Hello, World!" to the console window.

Console.ReadLine() The Console.ReadLine() method is used to read input from the user. It waits for the user to type something in the console window and press Enter, and then returns the input as a string. Here's an example:

```
153
154    Console.Write("Enter your name: ");
155    string name = Console.ReadLine();
156    Console.WriteLine("Hello, " + name + "!");
157
158
```

This code will output "Enter your name: " to the console window, wait for the user to enter their name, and then output "Hello, {name}!" to the console window, where {name} is the name that the user entered.

It's important to note that the Console.ReadLine() method returns a string, so if you want to use the input as a different data type (such as an integer or a double), you'll need to convert it using type conversion.

In summary, the Console class provides methods for input/output using the console window in C#. Console.WriteLine() is used to output text to the console, and Console.ReadLine() is used to read input from the user. These methods are fundamental to interacting with the user in a C# program.

Control Flow Statements

If statements

In programming, if statements are used to control the flow of a program based on a condition. In C#, the if statement is one of the most commonly used control structures.

The basic syntax of an if statement in C# is as follows:

```
159
160     if (condition)
161     {
162         // Code to execute if condition is true
163     }
164
```

The "condition" in the if statement is a Boolean expression that evaluates to true or false. If the condition is true, the code inside the curly braces will be executed. If the condition is false, the code inside the curly braces will be skipped.

Here's an example of using an if statement in C#:

```
167
168     int number = 5;
169     if (number > 0)
170     {
171         Console.WriteLine("The number is positive.");
172     }
173
```

In this example, the condition is "number > 0". If the value of "number" is greater than 0, the code inside the curly braces will be executed, which will output "The number is positive." to the console window.

If statements can also be combined with else and else if clauses to create more complex conditional logic. Here's an example:

```
176   int number = 5;
177   if (number > 0)
178   {
179       Console.WriteLine("The number is positive.");
180   }
181   else if (number < 0)
182   {
183       Console.WriteLine("The number is negative.");
184   }
185   else
186   {
187       Console.WriteLine("The number is zero.");
188   }
189
```

In this example, the program will first check if "number" is greater than 0. If it is, the program will output "The number is positive." to the console window. If it is not, the program will check if "number" is less than 0. If it is, the program will output "The number is negative." to the console window. If "number" is neither greater than nor less than 0, the program will output "The number is zero." to the console window.

In summary, if statements are used to control the flow of a program based on a condition in C#. They can be combined with else and else if clauses to create more complex conditional logic. If statements are a fundamental aspect of programming and are used in almost every program.

Switch statements

In C#, switch statements are used to control the flow of a program based on a value. They are a more concise and structured way of writing complex if/else statements. The basic syntax of a switch statement in C# is as follows:

```
192  switch (expression)
193  {
194      case value1:
195          // Code to execute if expression == value1
196          break;
197      case value2:
198          // Code to execute if expression == value2
199          break;
200      default:
201          // Code to execute if expression is not equal to any of the
202          //case values
203          break;
204  }
```

In this syntax, "expression" is the value to be tested, and each "case" represents a possible value of the expression. If the expression matches a case value, the code block associated with that case is executed. If the expression does not match any case value, the code block associated with the "default" case is executed.

Here's an example of using a switch statement in C#:

```
210  int dayOfWeek = 3;
211  string dayName;
212  switch (dayOfWeek)
213  {
214      case 1:
215          dayName = "Monday";
216          break;
217      case 2:
218          dayName = "Tuesday";
219          break;
220      case 3:
221          dayName = "Wednesday";
222          break;
223      case 4:
224          dayName = "Thursday";
225          break;
226      case 5:
227          dayName = "Friday";
228          break;
229      default:
230          dayName = "Weekend";
231          break;
232  }
233  Console.WriteLine("Today is " + dayName + ".");
234
```

In this example, the value of "dayOfWeek" is 3, so the code block associated with the "case 3" label will be executed. This will assign the value "Wednesday" to the "dayName" variable, and the program will output "Today is Wednesday." to the console window.

It's important to note that each case value must be unique, and the break statement is used to exit the switch statement after executing the code block associated with a case.

In Summary switch statements are used to control the flow of a program based on a value in C#. They provide a more concise and structured way of writing complex if/else statements. Switch statements are a fundamental aspect of programming and are used in many programs.

Loops (while, do-while, for)

In programming, loops are used to execute a block of code repeatedly until a certain condition is met. In C#, there are three types of loops: the while loop, the do-while loop, and the for loop.

The While Loop The while loop is used to execute a block of code repeatedly while a condition is true. The basic syntax of a while loop in C# is as follows:

```
238    while (condition)
239    {
240        // Code to execute while condition is true
241    }
242
243
```

In this syntax, "condition" is the Boolean expression that determines whether the loop should continue. The code inside the curly braces will be executed repeatedly while the condition is true.

Here's an example of using a while loop in C# to print the numbers from 1 to 5:

```
244
245     int i = 1;
246     while (i <= 5)
247     {
248         Console.WriteLine(i);
249         i++;
250     }
251
```

In this example, the loop will continue as long as the value of "i" is less than or equal to 5. The program will output the values 1, 2, 3, 4, and 5 to the console window.

The Do-While Loop The do-while loop is similar to the while loop, but the code inside the loop is executed at least once, even if the condition is initially false. The basic syntax of a do-while loop in C# is as follows:

```
253
254     do
255     {
256         // Code to execute at least once
257     } while (condition);
258
259
```

In this syntax, the code inside the curly braces will be executed at least once, and then the condition will be checked. If the condition is true, the code inside the curly braces will be executed again.

Here's an example of using a do-while loop in C# to print the numbers from 1 to 5:

```
260
261     int i = 1;
262     do
263     {
264         Console.WriteLine(i);
265         i++;
266     } while (i <= 5);
267
```

In this example, the loop will continue until the value of "i" is greater than 5. The program will output the values 1, 2, 3, 4, and 5 to the console window.

The For Loop The for loop is used to execute a block of code a specific number of times. The basic syntax of a for loop in C# is as follows:

```
for (initialization; condition; increment/decrement)
{
    // Code to execute while condition is true
}
```

In this syntax, "initialization" is an expression that initializes the loop counter, "condition" is the Boolean expression that determines whether the loop should continue, and "increment/decrement" is an expression that modifies the loop counter after each iteration.

Here's an example of using a for loop in C# to print the numbers from 1 to 5:

```
for (int i = 1; i <= 5; i++)
{
    Console.WriteLine(i);
}
```

In this example, the loop will continue until the value of "i" is greater than 5. The program will output the values 1, 2, 3, 4, and 5 to the console window.

fundamental concept in programming, and are essential for building algorithms and solving problems efficiently. Understanding how to use loops effectively is an important skill for any programmer.

When writing loops in C#, it's important to be mindful of the loop condition and the variables used in the loop. Incorrect loop conditions or improper variable use can lead to infinite loops, which can cause the program to crash or become unresponsive.

In addition to while, do-while, and for loops, C# also provides a range of control statements that can be used to modify the behavior of loops. These include the break statement, which terminates a loop early, and the continue statement, which skips the remaining code in a loop iteration and moves on to the next iteration.

Overall, loops are an important tool for any programmer to have in their toolbox. By understanding how to use while, do-while, and for loops effectively, and by being aware of the potential pitfalls of looping, developers can write more efficient and robust programs.

Using break and continue statements

In C#, the **break** and **continue** statements are used to control the flow of loops.

1. The Break Statement: The **break** statement is used to terminate a loop prematurely. When the **break** statement is encountered inside a loop, the loop is immediately exited, and the program execution resumes with the statement following the loop.

Here's an example of using a **break** statement in a **while** loop to exit the loop when the value of **i** is 5:

```
int i = 0;
while (i < 10)
{
    i++;
    if (i == 5)
    {
        break;
    }
    Console.WriteLine(i);
}
```

In this example, the loop will iterate over the values 1 through 5, and then exit the loop when the value of **i** is 5.

The Continue Statement: The **continue** statement is used to skip the current iteration of a loop and move on to the next iteration. When the **continue** statement is encountered inside a loop, the remaining code in the current iteration is skipped, and the loop moves on to the next iteration.

Here's an example of using a **continue** statement in a **for** loop to skip over even numbers:

```
296
297     for (int i = 1; i <= 10; i++)
298     {
299         if (i % 2 == 0)
300         {
301             continue;
302         }
303         Console.WriteLine(i);
304     }
305
```

In this example, the loop will print only the odd numbers from 1 to 10, by skipping over the even numbers with the **continue** statement.

In summary, the **break** and **continue** statements are powerful tools for controlling the flow of loops in C#. The **break** statement is used to terminate a loop prematurely, while the **continue** statement is used to skip the current iteration of a loop and move on to the next iteration. By using these statements effectively, developers can write more efficient and robust code.

2

Object-Oriented Programming

Object-oriented programming (OOP) is a programming paradigm that is based on the concept of objects, which can contain data and methods (functions) that operate on that data. In OOP, programs are designed by creating classes, which are templates for objects that define their properties (data) and behaviors (methods). Objects are then created from these classes, and can interact with each other to perform complex operations.

The key concepts in OOP include encapsulation, inheritance, and polymorphism. Encapsulation is the idea of bundling data and methods together into a single unit (class), and controlling access to that data and methods through access modifiers. Inheritance is the idea of creating new classes that are derived from existing classes, and that inherit the properties and methods of those classes. Polymorphism is the idea of using a single interface (method name) to represent multiple forms (implementations) of that method.

Classes and objects

In C#, a class is a blueprint for creating objects that share common properties and behaviors. An object is an instance of a class, and can have its own unique values for the class properties.

To define a class in C#, you use the **class** keyword, followed by the name of the class. Here's an example of a simple class definition:

```
class Person
{
    public string name;
    public int age;

    public void SayHello()
    {
        Console.WriteLine("Hello, my name is " + name
                        + " and I am " + age + " years old.");
    }
}
```

In this example, we define a **Person** class with two public properties (**name** and **age**) and one public method (**SayHello()**). The **name** property is of type **string**, and the **age** property is of type **int**. The **SayHello()** method writes a greeting to the console that includes the **name** and **age** properties.

To create an instance of the **Person** class, you use the **new** keyword, followed by the name of the class and any arguments required by the class constructor (if any). Here's an example of creating two **Person** objects and calling the **SayHello()** method on each object:

```
Person person1 = new Person();
person1.name = "Alice";
person1.age = 25;
person1.SayHello();

Person person2 = new Person();
person2.name = "Bob";
person2.age = 30;
person2.SayHello();
```

In this example, we create two **Person** objects (**person1** and **person2**) and set their **name** and **age** properties. We then call the **SayHello()** method on each object, which writes a greeting to the console that includes the **name** and **age** properties.

In summary, classes and objects are a fundamental concept in object-oriented programming (OOP), and allow developers to encapsulate data and behavior into reusable components. In C#, a class is a blueprint for creating objects, and an object is an instance of a class. To define a class, you use the **class** keyword, and to create an object, you use the **new** keyword. Classes can have properties and methods, which are accessed using dot notation.

Encapsulation

Encapsulation is one of the fundamental concepts in object-oriented programming (OOP). It refers to the practice of bundling data and the methods that operate on that data into a single unit (a class), and controlling access to that data and methods through access modifiers.

In C#, there are three access modifiers: **public**, **private**, and **protected**.

- **public** access modifier: A **public** property or method can be accessed from anywhere in the program, including outside of the class in which it is defined.

```
26
27    public class Person
28    {
29        public string name;
30
31        public void SayHello()
32        {
33            Console.WriteLine("Hello, my name is " + name + ".");
34        }
35    }
36
```

In this example, the **name** property and the **SayHello()** method are both declared as **public**, which means they can be accessed from anywhere in the program.

- **private** access modifier: A **private** property or method can only be accessed within the class in which it is defined.

```
37
38   public class BankAccount
39   {
40       private decimal balance;
41
42       public void Deposit(decimal amount)
43       {
44           balance += amount;
45       }
46
47       public decimal GetBalance()
48       {
49           return balance;
50       }
51   }
```

In this example, the **balance** property is declared as **private**, which means it can only be accessed from within the **BankAccount** class. The **Deposit()** and **GetBalance()** methods are both declared as **public**, which means they can be accessed from anywhere in the program.

- **protected** access modifier: A **protected** property or method can only be accessed within the class in which it is defined, or by a child class that inherits from that class.

```
53   public class Animal
54   {
55       protected string name;
56   }
57
58   public class Dog : Animal
59   {
60       public void SetName(string name)
61       {
62           this.name = name;
63       }
64   }
65
```

In this example, the **name** property is declared as **protected**, which means it can be accessed from within the **Animal** class and any child classes that inherit from the **Animal** class. The **SetName()** method is defined in the **Dog** class, which is a child class of the **Animal** class. The **SetName()** method can access the **name** property because it inherits from the **Animal** class.

In summary, encapsulation is an important concept in OOP that allows developers to control access to data and methods. By using access modifiers to restrict access to properties and methods, developers can ensure that their code is more secure, reliable, and maintainable.

Inheritance and polymorphism

Inheritance and polymorphism are two key concepts in object-oriented programming (OOP) that allow developers to create more efficient and modular code.

Inheritance is the process by which one class inherits the properties and methods of another class. The class that inherits from another class is called the child or derived class, and the class that is inherited from is called the parent or base class. In C#, you can define a class that inherits from another class using the colon (:) symbol. Here's an example of a **Child** class that inherits from a **Parent** class:

```
67   class Parent
68   {
69       public void SayHello()
70       {
71           Console.WriteLine("Hello from the parent class.");
72       }
73   }
74
75   class Child : Parent
76   {
77       public void SayGoodbye()
78       {
79           Console.WriteLine("Goodbye from the child class.");
80       }
81   }
82
```

In this example, we define a **Parent** class with a **SayHello()** method, and a **Child** class that inherits from the **Parent** class and has its own **SayGoodbye()** method. The **Child** class can access the **SayHello()** method of the **Parent** class using the **base** keyword.

Polymorphism is the ability of objects to take on multiple forms. In C#, polymorphism is achieved through method overriding and method overloading. Method overriding is the process by which a child class provides a specific implementation of a method that is already provided by its parent class. Method overloading is the process by which multiple methods with the same name but different parameters are defined in a class. Here's an example of method overriding and method overloading in a **Shape** class hierarchy:

```
class Shape
{
    public virtual void Draw()
    {
        Console.WriteLine("Drawing a shape.");
    }
}

class Circle : Shape
{
    public override void Draw()
    {
        Console.WriteLine("Drawing a circle.");
    }

    public void Draw(int size)
    {
        Console.WriteLine("Drawing a circle with size " + size + ".");
    }
}
```

In this example, we define a **Shape** class with a virtual **Draw()** method, and a **Circle** class that overrides the **Draw()** method and provides its own implementation. The **Circle** class also has an overloaded **Draw()** method that takes an integer argument.

In summary, inheritance and polymorphism are important concepts in object-oriented programming that allow developers to create more efficient and modular code. Inheritance allows classes to inherit the properties and

33

methods of other classes, while polymorphism allows objects to take on multiple forms through method overriding and method overloading.

Interfaces and abstract classes

Interfaces and abstract classes are two important concepts in object-oriented programming that allow developers to create more modular and reusable code.

An interface is a collection of abstract methods (methods without implementation) that define a contract between two objects. In C#, an interface is defined using the **interface** keyword. Here's an example of an interface that defines a contract for an object that can be serialized:

```
public interface ISerializable
{
    void Serialize();
    void Deserialize();
}
```

In this example, the **ISerializable** interface defines two methods: **Serialize()** and **Deserialize()**. Any class that implements this interface must provide an implementation for these methods.

An abstract class is a class that cannot be instantiated, but can be inherited from. An abstract class can contain abstract methods (methods without implementation) and concrete methods (methods with implementation). In C#, an abstract class is defined using the **abstract** keyword. Here's an example of an abstract class that defines a basic shape:

```
113
114    public abstract class Shape
115    {
116        public abstract double GetArea();
117        public abstract double GetPerimeter();
118
119        public void PrintDetails()
120        {
121            Console.WriteLine("Area: " + GetArea());
122            Console.WriteLine("Perimeter: " + GetPerimeter());
123        }
124    }
125
```

In this example, the **Shape** class is defined as abstract, and contains two abstract methods: **GetArea()** and **GetPerimeter()**. Any class that inherits from the **Shape** class must provide an implementation for these methods. The **Shape** class also contains a concrete method **PrintDetails()**, which can be used by any class that inherits from the **Shape** class.

In summary, interfaces and abstract classes are important concepts in object-oriented programming that allow developers to create more modular and reusable code. Interfaces define a contract between two objects, while abstract classes provide a template for other classes to inherit from. By using interfaces and abstract classes, developers can create code that is more flexible, maintainable, and extensible over time.

Constructors and destructors

Constructors and destructors are special methods in C# that are used to initialize and destroy objects, respectively.

A constructor is a method that is called when an object of a class is created. It is used to set initial values for the object's properties or perform any other initialization tasks. In C#, a constructor has the same name as the class and is defined using the **constructor** keyword. Here's an example of a constructor for a **Person** class:

```
126    public class Person
127    {
128        public string Name { get; set; }
129        public int Age { get; set; }
130
131        public Person(string name, int age)
132        {
133            Name = name;
134            Age = age;
135        }
136    }
137
```

In this example, the **Person** class has a constructor that takes two parameters (**name** and **age**) and initializes the **Name** and **Age** properties.

A destructor, on the other hand, is a method that is called when an object is destroyed or garbage collected. It is used to perform any cleanup tasks, such as releasing unmanaged resources or closing open files. In C#, a destructor is defined using the ~ character followed by the class name. Here's an example of a destructor for a **FileReader** class:

```
137
138    public class FileReader
139    {
140        private StreamReader reader;
141
142        public FileReader(string filename)
143        {
144            reader = new StreamReader(filename);
145        }
146
147        ~FileReader()
148        {
149            if (reader != null)
150            {
151                reader.Close();
152            }
153        }
154    }
155
```

In this example, the **FileReader** class has a constructor that takes a **filename** parameter and creates a new **StreamReader** object. The class also has a destructor that checks if the **reader** object is not null and closes it if it is open.

In summary, constructors and destructors are special methods in C# that are used to initialize and destroy objects, respectively. Constructors are called when an object is created, and destructors are called when an object is destroyed or garbage collected. By using constructors and destructors, developers can ensure that their objects are properly initialized and cleaned up, which can lead to more robust and reliable code.

Garbage collection

Garbage collection is an automatic memory management feature in C# that automatically frees up memory that is no longer being used by the program. Garbage collection helps prevent memory leaks and reduces the risk of crashes and other errors caused by running out of memory.

In C#, the garbage collector runs periodically and identifies memory that is no longer being used by the program. It then frees up this memory by removing it from the program's memory pool. The garbage collector uses a number of algorithms to determine which memory is no longer being used, such as reference counting and mark-and-sweep.

Developers can also manually release memory using the **Dispose()** method, which is commonly used with objects that manage unmanaged resources, such as files or network connections. The **Dispose()** method is typically called when an object is no longer needed, and it releases any resources that the object is holding onto.

Here's an example of using the **Dispose()** method to release unmanaged resources:

```
156
157    public class FileReader : IDisposable
158    {
159        private StreamReader reader;
160
161        public FileReader(string filename)
162        {
163            reader = new StreamReader(filename);
164        }
165
166        public void Dispose()
167        {
168            if (reader != null)
169            {
170                reader.Dispose();
171            }
172        }
173    }
```

In this example, the **FileReader** class implements the **IDisposable** interface, which requires it to have a **Dispose()** method. The **Dispose()** method checks if the **reader** object is not null and calls its **Dispose()** method to release any unmanaged resources.

In summary, garbage collection is an important feature in C# that helps manage memory automatically. By periodically freeing up memory that is no longer being used, garbage collection helps prevent memory leaks and reduces the risk of crashes and other errors caused by running out of memory. Developers can also manually release memory using the **Dispose()** method, which is commonly used with objects that manage unmanaged resources.

3

C# Language Features

C# is a powerful and flexible programming language that includes a wide range of features to help developers create robust and efficient applications. Here are some of the key language features in C#:

1. Delegates and events: Delegates are type-safe function pointers that can be used to pass methods as arguments to other methods or to store references to methods. Events are a way for an object to notify other objects when something interesting happens.
2. Generics: Generics allow developers to write code that can work with a variety of data types, without having to rewrite the code for each data type.
3. Lambda expressions: Lambda expressions are a concise way to write anonymous methods that can be used to perform simple tasks or as arguments to other methods.
4. LINQ (Language Integrated Query): LINQ is a set of language extensions that allow developers to query and manipulate data from different data sources using a uniform syntax.
5. Asynchronous programming with async/await: Asynchronous programming allows developers to write code that can run in the background without blocking the main thread, improving performance and responsiveness. The **async** and **await** keywords in C# make it easy to write

asynchronous code.

6. Reflection and attributes: Reflection allows developers to inspect and manipulate the metadata of types, objects, and assemblies at runtime. Attributes are metadata that can be attached to types, methods, and other elements of a program to provide additional information about them.

By using these language features, developers can write more efficient, modular, and extensible code in C#. They can also take advantage of libraries and frameworks that use these features to provide powerful and flexible functionality.

Delegates and events

Delegates and events are important concepts in C# that allow developers to create more flexible and modular code.

A delegate is a type that represents a method signature (the return type and parameter types of a method). It can be used to pass methods as arguments to other methods or to store references to methods. In C#, a delegate is defined using the **delegate** keyword. Here's an example of a delegate that represents a method that takes two integers and returns an integer:

```
public delegate int MathOperation(int x, int y);
```

In this example, the **MathOperation** delegate represents a method that takes two integers and returns an integer. Any method that matches this signature can be assigned to a variable of type **MathOperation**.

An event is a way for an object to notify other objects when something interesting happens. In C#, an event is defined using the **event** keyword. Here's an example of an event that is raised when a button is clicked:

```
 5
 6    public class Button
 7    {
 8        public event EventHandler Click;
 9
10        public void OnClick()
11        {
12            if (Click != null)
13            {
14                Click(this, EventArgs.Empty);
15            }
16        }
17    }
18
```

In this example, the **Button** class has an event called **Click**, which is raised when the **OnClick()** method is called. Other objects can subscribe to this event by adding a method to the event's invocation list using the += operator. When the **OnClick()** method is called, all methods in the invocation list are called.

Here's an example of using delegates and events to create a simple calculator:

```
37   public class Program
38   {
39       static int Add(int x, int y)
40       {
41           return x + y;
42       }
43
44       static int Multiply(int x, int y)
45       {
46           return x * y;
47       }
48
49       static void Main(string[] args)
50       {
51           Calculator calculator = new Calculator();
52           calculator.Operation += Add;
53           calculator.Operation += Multiply;
54
55           int result1 = calculator.Calculate(5, 3); // 8
56           int result2 = calculator.Calculate(5, 2); // 10
57
58           Console.WriteLine("Result 1: " + result1);
59           Console.WriteLine("Result 2: " + result2);
60       }
61   }
62
```

In this example, the **Calculator** class has an event called **Operation**, which is raised when the **Calculate()** method is called. The **Main()** method subscribes two methods (**Add** and **Multiply**) to the **Operation** event, which are used to perform addition and multiplication. When the **Calculate()** method is called, it invokes the **Operation** event, which calls all subscribed methods. The **Main()** method then prints the results of the calculations.

In summary, delegates and events are important concepts in C# that allow developers to create more flexible and modular code. Delegates can be used to pass methods as arguments to other methods or to store references to methods. Events can be used to notify other objects when something interesting happens. By using delegates and events, developers can create code that is more modular, extensible, and maintainable.

Generics is a powerful feature in C# that allows developers to create reusable code that can work with a variety of data types, without having to rewrite the code for each data type. Generics can improve code efficiency, reduce errors, and enhance code readability.

In C#, generic code is defined using type parameters, which are specified in angle brackets (< >). Here's an example of a generic method that swaps two values of any type:

```
63
64    public static void Swap<T>(ref T a, ref T b)
65    {
66        T temp = a;
67        a = b;
68        b = temp;
69    }
70
```

In this example, the **Swap** method has a type parameter **T** that specifies the type of the values to be swapped. The **ref** keyword is used to pass the values by reference, so that the original values are modified.

Here's an example of using the **Swap** method to swap two integers:

```
72
73    int a = 5;
74    int b = 10;
75    Swap<int>(ref a, ref b);
76
```

In this example, the **Swap** method is called with the **int** type parameter to swap the values of **a** and **b**.

Generics

Generics can also be used to create generic classes, interfaces, and delegates. Here's an example of a generic class that represents a stack of any type:

```
78
79    public class Stack<T>
80    {
81        private List<T> items = new List<T>();
82
83        public void Push(T item)
84        {
85            items.Add(item);
86        }
87
88        public T Pop()
89        {
90            if (items.Count == 0)
91            {
92                throw new InvalidOperationException("Stack is empty");
93            }
94            T item = items[items.Count - 1];
95            items.RemoveAt(items.Count - 1);
96            return item;
97        }
98    }
```

In this example, the **Stack** class has a type parameter **T** that specifies the type of the items in the stack. The class has two methods, **Push** and **Pop**, that add and remove items from the stack.

Here's an example of using the **Stack** class to create a stack of integers:

```
100
101    Stack<int> stack = new Stack<int>();
102    stack.Push(1);
103    stack.Push(2);
104    int x = stack.Pop(); // x is 2
105
```

In this example, a **Stack** object is created with the **int** type parameter, and two integers are pushed onto the stack. The **Pop** method is then called to remove the top item from the stack and assign it to the variable **x**.

In summary, generics is a powerful feature in C# that allows developers to write reusable code that can work with a variety of data types. By using type parameters, developers can create generic methods, classes, interfaces, and delegates that can improve code efficiency, reduce errors, and enhance code readability.

Lambda expressions

Lambda expressions are a powerful feature in C# that allow developers to write concise, anonymous methods that can be used to perform simple tasks or as arguments to other methods. Lambda expressions can improve code readability and reduce the amount of code that needs to be written.

A lambda expression is defined using the => operator, which separates the input parameters from the expression that performs the task. Here's an example of a lambda expression that multiplies two numbers:

```
107
108    Func<int, int, int> multiply = (x, y) => x * y;
109
```

In this example, the **multiply** variable is defined as a delegate of type **Func<int, int, int>**, which represents a method that takes two integers as input and returns an integer as output. The lambda expression **(x, y) => x * y** is assigned to the **multiply** variable, which multiplies the two input numbers.

Lambda expressions can also be used as arguments to other methods. Here's an example of using a lambda expression to sort a list of strings:

```
110
111    List<string> names = new List<string> { "Alice", "Bob", "Charlie", "Dave" };
112    names.Sort((x, y) => x.Length.CompareTo(y.Length));
113
```

In this example, the **Sort** method of the **List<string>** class is called with a lambda expression that compares the length of two strings. The lambda expression **(x, y) => x.Length.CompareTo(y.Length)** takes two strings as input and compares their lengths using the **CompareTo** method.

Lambda expressions can also be used to create more complex expressions using LINQ (Language Integrated Query), which is a set of language extensions that allow developers to query and manipulate data from different data sources using a uniform syntax. Here's an example of using a lambda expression with

LINQ to filter a list of numbers:

```
114
115    List<int> numbers = new List<int> { 1, 2, 3, 4, 5 };
116    var evenNumbers = numbers.Where(n => n % 2 == 0);
117
```

In this example, the **Where** method of the **List<int>** class is called with a lambda expression that checks whether a number is even (**n % 2 == 0**). The **Where** method returns a new collection of the numbers that satisfy the condition.

In summary, lambda expressions are a powerful feature in C# that allow developers to write concise, anonymous methods that can be used to perform simple tasks or as arguments to other methods. By using lambda expressions, developers can improve code readability, reduce code duplication, and create more flexible and modular code.

LINQ (Language Integrated Query)

LINQ (Language Integrated Query) is a powerful feature in C# that allows developers to query and manipulate data from different data sources using a unified syntax. LINQ is based on a set of language extensions that provide a consistent way to access and manipulate data from a variety of sources, such as arrays, collections, databases, and XML.

LINQ uses a functional programming approach to query data, where queries are expressed as expressions and are composed of a series of operators that transform the data. Here's an example of using LINQ to query a list of numbers:

```
119
120    List<int> numbers = new List<int> { 1, 2, 3, 4, 5 };
121    var evenNumbers = from n in numbers
122                      where n % 2 == 0
123                      select n;
124
125
```

In this example, the **from** keyword is used to define a range variable **n** that represents each element in the **numbers** list. The **where** keyword is used to filter the numbers that are even, and the **select** keyword is used to select the even numbers. The result is a new collection of even numbers.

LINQ also provides a set of standard query operators that can be used to perform common operations, such as filtering, sorting, grouping, aggregating, and joining data. Here's an example of using LINQ to group a list of products by category:

```
125
126    List<Product> products = new List<Product> {
127        new Product { Name = "Apples", Category = "Fruit", Price = 1.99 },
128        new Product { Name = "Bananas", Category = "Fruit", Price = 2.99 },
129        new Product { Name = "Cheese", Category = "Dairy", Price = 5.99 },
130        new Product { Name = "Milk", Category = "Dairy", Price = 2.49 }
131    };
132    var groupedProducts = from p in products
133                          group p by p.Category into g
134                          select new { Category = g.Key, Products = g };
```

In this example, the **group by** keyword is used to group the products by category, and the **select** keyword is used to select the category and the products in each group. The result is a new collection of anonymous objects that contain the category and the products in each group.

LINQ also supports method syntax, which is a more concise and fluent way of writing LINQ queries using method calls instead of query expressions. Here's an example of using method syntax to perform the same query as the previous example:

```
136
137    var groupedProducts = products
138        .GroupBy(p => p.Category)
139        .Select(g => new { Category = g.Key, Products = g });
140
```

In this example, the **GroupBy** method is used to group the products by category, and the **Select** method is used to select the category and the products in each group.

In summary, LINQ is a powerful feature in C# that allows developers to query and manipulate data from different data sources using a unified syntax. By using LINQ, developers can write more concise, expressive, and flexible code that can work with a variety of data sources. LINQ is a key feature in C# that helps developers to build efficient, scalable, and maintainable applications.

Asynchronous programming

Asynchronous programming is a programming technique that allows a program to perform multiple tasks concurrently, without blocking the main thread of execution. Asynchronous programming can improve the performance and responsiveness of an application, especially when dealing with long-running or I/O-bound operations.

C# provides several asynchronous programming features, such as the **async** and **await** keywords, which allow developers to write asynchronous code that is more readable and maintainable than traditional callback-based code.

The **async** keyword is used to mark a method as asynchronous, and the **await** keyword is used to wait for an asynchronous operation to complete. Here's an example of using **async** and **await** to download a file asynchronously:

```
142
143    async Task DownloadFileAsync(string url, string path)
144    {
145        using (var client = new WebClient())
146        {
147            await client.DownloadFileTaskAsync(url, path);
148        }
149    }
```

In this example, the **DownloadFileAsync** method is marked as asynchronous using the **async** keyword, and the **await** keyword is used to wait for the **DownloadFileTaskAsync** method to complete. The **DownloadFileTaskAsync** method is an asynchronous method provided by the **WebClient** class, which downloads a file from the specified URL and saves it to the specified path.

Asynchronous programming with **async** and **await** can also be used to execute multiple tasks concurrently. Here's an example of using **Task.WhenAll** to download multiple files concurrently:

```
151
152    async Task DownloadFilesAsync(string[] urls, string[] paths)
153    {
154        var tasks = new List<Task>();
155        for (int i = 0; i < urls.Length; i++)
156        {
157            tasks.Add(DownloadFileAsync(urls[i], paths[i]));
158        }
159        await Task.WhenAll(tasks);
160    }
```

In this example, the **DownloadFilesAsync** method uses a loop to create a list of **Task** objects, each representing an asynchronous operation to download a file. The **Task.WhenAll** method is used to wait for all the tasks to complete before returning.

Asynchronous programming with **async** and **await** can also be used with other programming features, such as LINQ and event handlers. For example, here's an example of using **async** and **await** with LINQ to perform a database query asynchronously:

```
162
163    async Task<List<Customer>> GetCustomersAsync()
164    {
165        using (var context = new MyDbContext())
166        {
167            var customers = from c in context.Customers
168                            where c.Country == "USA"
169                            select c;
170            return await customers.ToListAsync();
171        }
172    }
```

In this example, the LINQ query is performed asynchronously using the **ToListAsync** method, which returns a **Task<List<Customer>>**. The **await** keyword is used to wait for the query to complete, and the result is returned as a list of customers.

In summary, asynchronous programming with **async** and **await** is a powerful feature in C# that allows developers to write asynchronous code that is more readable, maintainable, and scalable than traditional callback-based code. Asynchronous programming can improve the performance and responsiveness of an application, especially when dealing with long-running or I/O-bound operations.

Reflection and attributes

Reflection and attributes are powerful features in C# that allow developers to inspect and manipulate the metadata of types, objects, and assemblies at runtime. Reflection enables the examination of metadata in order to obtain type information at runtime, while attributes provide a way to add declarative information to code, which can be used by the runtime to control the behavior of the application.

Reflection can be used to dynamically create objects, invoke methods, access fields and properties, and perform other operations on types and objects. Here's an example of using reflection to create an instance of a class and invoke a method:

```
174
175    Type type = typeof(MyClass);
176    object instance = Activator.CreateInstance(type);
177    MethodInfo method = type.GetMethod("MyMethod");
178    method.Invoke(instance, null);
179
```

In this example, the **typeof** keyword is used to obtain a **Type** object that represents the **MyClass** type. The **Activator.CreateInstance** method is used to create an instance of the **MyClass** type. The **GetMethod** method is used to obtain a **MethodInfo** object that represents the **MyMethod** method. The **Invoke** method is used to invoke the **MyMethod** method on the **MyClass** instance.

Attributes provide a way to add declarative information to code, which can be used by the runtime to control the behavior of the application. Attributes can be applied to types, methods, properties, fields, and other elements of the code. Here's an example of using an attribute to mark a method as obsolete:

```
179
180    class MyClass
181    {
182        [Obsolete("This method is obsolete. Use MyNewMethod instead.")]
183        public void MyMethod()
184        {
185            // ...
186        }
187    }
```

In this example, the **Obsolete** attribute is used to mark the **MyMethod** method as obsolete, and to provide a message that explains why the method is obsolete. The compiler and the runtime can use this attribute to generate warnings or errors when the method is used, and to suggest using the new method instead.

Reflection and attributes are powerful features in C# that can be used to add dynamic behavior and metadata to applications. However, they can also introduce complexity and performance overhead, and should be used judiciously.

4

Methods and Functions

In C#, a method is a block of code that performs a specific task. Methods are used to organize code into reusable units and to avoid duplication of code. Methods can take parameters as input, and can return a value as output.

A function is a type of method that returns a value. In C#, a function is defined using a return type, such as **int**, **double**, **string**, or any other valid data type.

Here's an example of a simple method that adds two numbers and returns the result:

```
2
3    int Add(int a, int b)
4    {
5        int result = a + b;
6        return result;
7    }
8
```

In this example, the **Add** method takes two **int** parameters, **a** and **b**, and returns an **int** value that represents the sum of the two parameters. The method body consists of a single statement that adds the two parameters and assigns the result to a local variable named **result**. The **return** statement is used to return the value of the **result** variable to the caller.

Methods can also be used to perform complex tasks that involve multiple statements and control structures. Here's an example of a method that calculates the factorial of a number using a **for** loop:

```
 9
10    int Factorial(int n)
11    {
12         int result = 1;
13         for (int i = 1; i <= n; i++)
14         {
15              result *= i;
16         }
17         return result;
18    }
19
```

In this example, the **Factorial** method takes an **int** parameter, **n**, and returns an **int** value that represents the factorial of the parameter. The method body consists of a **for** loop that iterates from 1 to **n** and multiplies the **result** variable by each value of **i** in turn. The **return** statement is used to return the value of the **result** variable to the caller.

In summary, methods and functions are important building blocks of C# programs. They allow code to be organized into reusable units, and provide a way to perform complex tasks and return results to the caller.

In C#, a method is defined using the **method** keyword, followed by the method name, the parameter list in parentheses, and the method body in curly braces. Here's an example of a simple method that prints a message to the console:

```
20
21    void PrintMessage(string message)
22    {
23         Console.WriteLine(message);
24    }
25
```

In this example, the **PrintMessage** method takes a **string** parameter named **message** and does not return a value (**void** return type). The method body consists of a single statement that calls the **Console.WriteLine** method to print the **message** parameter to the console.

Defining and calling methods

To call a method in C#, you need to provide the arguments (if any) that match the parameter list of the method. Here's an example of calling the **PrintMessage** method with a string argument:

```
26
27    PrintMessage("Hello, world!");
28
```

In this example, the **PrintMessage** method is called with a single string argument, **"Hello, world!"**. The method prints the message to the console.

Methods can also be called with multiple arguments and different data types. Here's an example of a method that calculates the sum of two numbers:

```
29
30    int Add(int a, int b)
31    {
32        int sum = a + b;
33        return sum;
34    }
35
36    // Calling the Add method with two integer arguments
37    int result = Add(2, 3);
38    Console.WriteLine(result); // Output: 5
39
```

In this example, the **Add** method takes two **int** parameters, **a** and **b**, and returns an **int** value that represents the sum of the two parameters. The method is called with two integer arguments, **2** and **3**, and the result is assigned to a variable named **result**. The **Console.WriteLine** method is used to print the result to the console.

In summary, defining and calling methods is an essential part of C# programming. Methods allow you to encapsulate complex logic into reusable units, which can improve the maintainability and readability of your code.

Calling methods from other methods

In C#, methods can call other methods to reuse code and perform complex tasks. To call a method from another method, you need to use the method name and provide the arguments that match the parameter list of the method.

Here's an example of a program that calls two methods to calculate the factorial of a number:

```
using System;

class Program
{
    static void Main()
    {
        int number = 5;
        int factorial = CalculateFactorial(number);
        PrintResult(number, factorial);
    }

    static int CalculateFactorial(int n)
    {
        int result = 1;
        for (int i = 1; i <= n; i++)
        {
            result *= i;
        }
        return result;
    }

    static void PrintResult(int n, int factorial)
    {
        Console.WriteLine("The factorial of {0} is {1}.", n, factorial);
    }
}
```

In this example, the **Main** method calls two other methods, **CalculateFactorial** and **PrintResult**. The **CalculateFactorial** method takes an integer parameter, **n**, and returns an integer value that represents the factorial of **n**. The

PrintResult method takes two integer parameters, **n** and **factorial**, and prints a message to the console that shows the result of the calculation.

The **Main** method declares an integer variable named **number** and initializes it to **5**. The method then calls the **CalculateFactorial** method with the **number** variable as an argument, and assigns the result to an integer variable named **factorial**. Finally, the **Main** method calls the **PrintResult** method with the **number** and **factorial** variables as arguments, to display the result to the console.

In summary, calling methods from other methods is a common practice in C# programming. It allows you to reuse code and organize your logic into smaller, more manageable units. When calling a method from another method, you need to provide the correct arguments that match the parameter list of the method.

Understanding method scope and visibility

In C#, methods have a scope that defines where they can be accessed in your program. The scope of a method is determined by its access modifier, which can be one of the following:

- **public**: The method is accessible from any code in the program.
- **private**: The method is only accessible from within the same class.
- **protected**: The method is accessible from within the same class and from derived classes.
- **internal**: The method is accessible from any code in the same assembly.
- **protected internal**: The method is accessible from within the same assembly and from derived classes.

Here's an example of a program that demonstrates method scope and visibility:

```
69    using System;
70
71    class Program
72    {
73        static void Main()
74        {
75            MyClass obj = new MyClass();
76            obj.PublicMethod();  // Can be accessed from Main
77            //obj.PrivateMethod();  // Cannot be accessed from Main
78            //obj.ProtectedMethod();  // Cannot be accessed from Main
79            //obj.InternalMethod();  // Cannot be accessed from Main
80            //obj.ProtectedInternalMethod();  // Cannot be accessed from Main
81        }
82    }
83
84    class MyClass
85    {
86        public void PublicMethod()
87        {
88            Console.WriteLine("This is a public method.");
89        }
90
91        private void PrivateMethod()
92        {
93            Console.WriteLine("This is a private method.");
94        }
95
96        protected void ProtectedMethod()
97        {
98            Console.WriteLine("This is a protected method.");
99        }
100
101       internal void InternalMethod()
102       {
103           Console.WriteLine("This is an internal method.");
104       }
105
106       protected internal void ProtectedInternalMethod()
107       {
108           Console.WriteLine("This is a protected internal method.");
109       }
110   }
```

In this example, the **Main** method is declared with the **static** modifier, which means it can be called without creating an instance of the **Program** class. The **Main** method creates an instance of the **MyClass** class and calls its **PublicMethod** method, which is declared with the **public** access modifier, so it can be accessed from **Main**.

The **MyClass** class contains five methods with different access modifiers. The **PrivateMethod** method is declared with the **private** access modifier, so it can only be accessed from within the same class. The **ProtectedMethod** method is declared with the **protected** access modifier, so it can be accessed from within the same class and from derived classes. The **InternalMethod**

method is declared with the **internal** access modifier, so it can be accessed from any code in the same assembly. The **ProtectedInternalMethod** method is declared with the **protected internal** access modifier, so it can be accessed from within the same assembly and from derived classes.

In summary, method scope and visibility in C# are determined by the access modifiers you use. Public methods can be accessed from any code in the program, while private methods can only be accessed from within the same class. Protected, internal, and protected internal methods have varying levels of accessibility depending on the context in which they are used.

Function overloading

In C#, you can define multiple methods with the same name, but different parameter lists. This is called function overloading, and it allows you to provide different versions of a method that perform similar operations on different types of data or with different numbers of arguments.

Here's an example of function overloading in C#:

```
using System;

class Program
{
    static void Main()
    {
        int result1 = Add(2, 3);
        double result2 = Add(2.5, 3.7);
        string result3 = Add("Hello, ", "world!");

        Console.WriteLine(result1);  // Output: 5
        Console.WriteLine(result2);  // Output: 6.2
        Console.WriteLine(result3);  // Output: Hello, world!
    }

    static int Add(int a, int b)
    {
        return a + b;
    }

    static double Add(double a, double b)
    {
        return a + b;
    }

    static string Add(string a, string b)
    {
        return a + b;
    }
}
```

In this example, the **Main** method calls three different versions of the **Add** method, each with a different parameter list. The first version takes two integer arguments and returns an integer value, while the second version takes two double arguments and returns a double value. The third version takes two string arguments and returns a string value that represents the concatenation of the two strings.

When you call a method that has multiple overloads, the C# compiler determines which version of the method to call based on the types and number of arguments you provide. In this example, the C# compiler knows to call the first version of the **Add** method with two integer arguments, the second version with two double arguments, and the third version with two string arguments.

In summary, function overloading in C# allows you to define multiple versions of a method that perform similar operations on different types of data or with different numbers of arguments. This can improve the flexibility and readability of your code by allowing you to use the same method name for different types of operations.

Method resolution and ambiguity

Method resolution and ambiguity refer to the process of determining which method to call when there are multiple methods with the same name and parameter lists in the same class or inheritance hierarchy.

In C#, method resolution and ambiguity are handled using a set of rules called the method resolution algorithm (MRA). The MRA takes into account the following factors:

- The exact types of the arguments passed to the method call.
- The number of arguments passed to the method call.
- The order of the arguments passed to the method call.
- The presence or absence of optional arguments.

Based on these factors, the MRA determines which method to call. If there is only one method that matches the given arguments, then that method is called. If there are multiple methods that match the given arguments, then the MRA applies a set of rules to determine which method to call.

Here's an example that illustrates method resolution and ambiguity in C#:

```
146    using System;
147
148    class Program
149    {
150        static void Main()
151        {
152            Console.WriteLine(Add(2, 3));        // Output: 5
153            Console.WriteLine(Add(2.5, 3.7));    // Output: 6.2
154        }
155
156        static int Add(int a, int b)
157        {
158            return a + b;
159        }
160
161        static double Add(double a, double b)
162        {
163            return a + b;
164        }
165
166        static string Add(string a, string b)
167        {
168            return a + b;
169        }
170    }
```

In this example, the **Main** method calls two different versions of the **Add** method: one that takes two integers and returns an integer, and one that takes two doubles and returns a double. When the first version of the **Add** method is called with two integers, the MRA determines that this method is the best match and calls it. When the second version of the **Add** method is called with two doubles, the MRA determines that this method is the best match and calls it.

In some cases, there may be multiple methods that match the given arguments equally well, and the MRA may not be able to determine which method to call. This is known as method ambiguity. In such cases, the C# compiler generates a compile-time error.

In summary, method resolution and ambiguity in C# refer to the process of determining which method to call when there are multiple methods with the same name and parameter lists in the same class or inheritance hierarchy. This is handled using the method resolution algorithm (MRA), which takes into account the types, number, order, and optionality of the arguments passed to the method call. If there is only one method that matches the given arguments, then that method is called. If there are multiple methods that match the given arguments equally well, then the C# compiler generates a compile-time error.

Passing parameters

In C#, a method can receive information from the calling code by passing parameters. A parameter is a variable that is declared in the method signature and is used to receive a value from the calling code.

Here's an example of a method that receives two integer parameters:

```
public static int Add(int a, int b)
{
    return a + b;
}
```

In this example, the **Add** method receives two integer parameters, **a** and **b**, and returns their sum.

When calling a method that takes parameters, you pass in the values to be assigned to those parameters. Here's an example of calling the **Add** method with two integer arguments:

```
int result = Add(3, 4);
```

In this example, the **Add** method is called with the integer values 3 and 4. The method returns their sum, which is assigned to the **result** variable.

C# supports several types of parameters, including:

- Value parameters: The most common type of parameter, which passes

the value of the argument to the method.
- Reference parameters: A type of parameter that allows a method to modify the value of the argument passed in.
- Output parameters: A type of parameter that allows a method to return a value in addition to its return value.
- Optional parameters: A type of parameter that has a default value assigned, so the caller can omit it.

To pass parameters to a method, you can specify them in the method call in the same order as they are declared in the method signature. You can also use named parameters to specify them out of order. For example:

```
181
182     int result = Add(b: 4, a: 3);
```

In this example, the parameters are specified out of order, with **b** before **a**. The result is still the same, because the named parameters are used to match the correct parameter in the method signature.

In summary, passing parameters is a way to provide information to a method in C#. Parameters are declared in the method signature, and can be specified in the method call either by position or by name. C# supports several types of parameters, including value, reference, output, and optional parameters.

Returning values

In C#, a method can return a value to the calling code using the **return** statement. The return value can be of any data type, including built-in types like **int**, **double**, and **string**, as well as custom types defined by classes.

Here's an example of a method that returns an integer value:

```
184
185    public static int Add(int a, int b)
186    {
187        return a + b;
188    }
```

In this example, the **Add** method takes two integer parameters, **a** and **b**, and returns their sum using the **return** statement.

When calling a method that returns a value, you can assign the returned value to a variable. Here's an example of calling the **Add** method and assigning the returned value to a variable:

```
190
191    int result = Add(3, 4);
192
```

In this example, the **Add** method is called with the integer values **3** and **4**. The returned value, which is the sum of **3** and **4**, is assigned to the **result** variable.

In addition to returning a value, a method can also have side effects, such as modifying a class member or printing output to the console. However, it's generally considered good practice to separate methods that return values from those that have side effects, to make the code easier to understand and maintain.

To define a method that returns a value in C#, you need to specify the return type in the method signature. For example:

```
193
194    public static string GetGreeting(string name)
195    {
196        return "Hello, " + name + "!";
197    }
198
```

In this example, the **GetGreeting** method takes a string parameter **name** and returns a string that contains a greeting using that name.

In summary, returning values is a way for a method to provide information to the calling code in C#. The **return** statement is used to specify the value to be returned. A method that returns a value must specify its return type in the method signature. When calling a method that returns a value, the returned value can be assigned to a variable or used directly in an expression.

Recursion

Recursion is a programming technique where a method calls itself to solve a problem. Recursive algorithms are often used when a problem can be broken down into smaller subproblems of the same type.

In C#, a recursive method is defined like any other method, but it calls itself within its own code. Here's an example of a recursive method that calculates the factorial of a number:

```
public static int Factorial(int n)
{
    if (n == 0)
    {
        return 1;
    }
    else
    {
        return n * Factorial(n - 1);
    }
}
```

In this example, the **Factorial** method takes an integer parameter **n** and returns the factorial of **n**. If **n** is 0, then the method returns 1 (because 0! = 1). Otherwise, it multiplies **n** by the factorial of **n-1**, which is calculated by calling the **Factorial** method recursively.

When calling a recursive method, it's important to ensure that the recursion eventually stops. In the **Factorial** method, the recursion stops when **n** is equal to 0, which is the base case of the recursion. If the base case is never reached, then the method will continue calling itself indefinitely, which can lead to a stack overflow error.

Here's an example of calling the **Factorial** method:

```
214    int result = Factorial(5); // result = 5 * 4 * 3 * 2 * 1 = 120
215
```

In this example, the **Factorial** method is called with the integer value **5**. The method calculates the factorial of **5** by recursively calling itself with decreasing values of **n**, until it reaches the base case of **n = 0**. The returned value, which is the factorial of **5**, is assigned to the **result** variable.

In summary, recursion is a programming technique where a method calls itself to solve a problem. Recursive algorithms are often used when a problem can be broken down into smaller subproblems of the same type. In C#, a recursive method is defined like any other method, but it calls itself within its own code. Recursive methods must have a base case that stops the recursion, to avoid infinite recursion.

5

Arrays and Collections

Arrays and collections are important data structures in C# that allow you to store and manipulate groups of related data items.

Arrays are fixed-size collections of elements of the same data type, and are used to store a group of values that are accessed by an index. They are useful for performing operations on a group of related values, such as calculating the sum or average of a set of numbers.

Collections, on the other hand, are more flexible and dynamic than arrays, and can grow or shrink in size as needed. They are made up of individual elements, each of which can have a different data type, and are commonly used to store and manipulate groups of related objects.

C# provides a range of collection classes, including lists, dictionaries, queues, and stacks, each with its own specific functionality and characteristics. These collection classes offer a range of powerful features and methods that enable efficient manipulation of data, such as searching, sorting, and filtering.

Both arrays and collections are essential tools for developers, and a thorough understanding of their usage and capabilities is essential for building efficient and effective C# applications.

Declaring and initializing arrays

In C#, arrays are used to store a fixed-size collection of elements of the same data type. Declaring and initializing an array involves the following steps:

1. Declare the array variable: You first need to declare a variable that will hold the array. This is done by specifying the data type of the elements followed by a set of square brackets [].
2. For example: **int[] myArray;**
3. Initialize the array: Once the array variable is declared, you can initialize it by assigning a set of values to it. There are two ways to initialize an array:
4. a. Initializing with a set of values: You can initialize an array by providing a set of values enclosed in curly braces {} separated by commas.
5. For example: **int[] myArray = { 1, 2, 3, 4, 5 };**
6. b. Initializing with a specified size: You can also initialize an array with a specified size by using the new keyword followed by the data type and the size of the array enclosed in square brackets [].
7. For example: **int[] myArray = new int[5];**
8. Accessing array elements: You can access individual elements in an array by using their index value. Array indices start at 0, so the first element of an array is at index 0, the second element is at index 1, and so on.
9. For example: **int firstElement = myArray[0];**

Overall, declaring and initializing arrays is an essential skill for C# developers, as arrays are a fundamental data structure that is used extensively in C# programming.

Array operations (sorting, searching, copying)

Arrays are a key data structure in C# and can be used to store a collection of values of the same data type. Once an array is created and initialized, there are several common operations that can be performed on it, such as sorting, searching, and copying.

Sorting an array: To sort an array in C#, you can use the Array.Sort method. This method sorts the elements of an array in ascending order. For example:

```
2
3    int[] myArray = {5, 3, 2, 8, 1};
4    Array.Sort(myArray);
5
```

After calling the **Array.Sort** method, the **myArray** will be sorted in ascending order: {1, 2, 3, 5, 8}.

Searching an array: To search for a specific element in an array, you can use the Array.IndexOf method. This method searches for the specified value and returns its index if found. If the value is not found, the method returns -1. For example:

```
6
7    int[] myArray = {5, 3, 2, 8, 1};
8    int index = Array.IndexOf(myArray, 8);
9
```

After calling the **Array.IndexOf** method with the value 8, the **index** variable will contain the value 4, which is the index of the value 8 in the **myArray**.

Copying an array: To copy an array in C#, you can use the Array.Copy method. This method creates a new array with the same size and elements as the original array. For example:

```
10
11    int[] myArray = {5, 3, 2, 8, 1};
12    int[] newArray = new int[5];
13    Array.Copy(myArray, newArray, 5);
```

After calling the **Array.Copy** method, the **newArray** will have the same values as **myArray**: {5, 3, 2, 8, 1}.

Overall, these common array operations are important tools for C# developers, and a thorough understanding of how to perform them is essential for working with arrays effectively in C#.

Lists, dictionaries, and other collections

In C#, collections are used to store and manipulate groups of related data. The .NET framework provides several built-in collection classes, such as lists, dictionaries, and queues, which offer a wide range of functionality and flexibility.

Lists: Lists are dynamic collections of objects that can be accessed by index. They are similar to arrays but can be resized at runtime. In C#, you can create a list using the List<T> class, where T is the data type of the elements in the list. For example:

```
15
16    List<int> myNumbers = new List<int>();
17    myNumbers.Add(5);
18    myNumbers.Add(10);
```

In this example, a new List<int> is created and initialized with two elements, 5 and 10. The Add method is used to add new elements to the list.

Dictionaries: Dictionaries are collections that store key-value pairs. In C#, you can create a dictionary using the Dictionary<TKey, TValue> class, where TKey is the data type of the keys and TValue is the data type of the values. For example:

```
20
21    Dictionary<string, int> myDictionary = new Dictionary<string, int>();
22    myDictionary.Add("one", 1);
23    myDictionary.Add("two", 2);
```

In this example, a new Dictionary<string, int> is created and initialized with two key-value pairs, "one": 1 and "two": 2. The Add method is used to add new key-value pairs to the dictionary.

Using other collection classes

In addition to lists and dictionaries, the .NET framework provides other collection classes that can be useful for specific scenarios.

Stack: The Stack<T> class is used to implement a last-in, first-out (LIFO) data structure. It provides methods such as Push(), Pop(), and Peek() for adding and removing items from the stack. For example:

```
26    Stack<int> myStack = new Stack<int>();
27    myStack.Push(1);
28    myStack.Push(2);
29    myStack.Push(3);
30    int topItem = myStack.Pop(); // topItem is now 3
31
```

Queue: The Queue<T> class is used to implement a first-in, first-out (FIFO) data structure. It provides methods such as Enqueue(), Dequeue(), and Peek() for adding and removing items from the queue. For example:

```
32
33    Queue<string> myQueue = new Queue<string>();
34    myQueue.Enqueue("apple");
35    myQueue.Enqueue("banana");
36    myQueue.Enqueue("orange");
37    string firstItem = myQueue.Dequeue(); // firstItem is now "apple"
38
```

HashSet: The HashSet<T> class is used to store a collection of unique items. It provides methods such as Add(), Remove(), and Contains() for working with the set. For example:

```
39
40    HashSet<int> mySet = new HashSet<int>();
41    mySet.Add(1);
42    mySet.Add(2);
43    mySet.Add(3);
44    mySet.Add(3); // this will not add a new item to the set,
45                  //since 3 is already in the set
46
47
```

71

By using these collection classes, you can create data structures that are optimized for specific scenarios and operations. It's important to choose the right collection class for the job, in order to achieve the best performance and functionality.

Understanding collection interfaces

In C#, collection interfaces provide a standardized way of working with different types of collections, regardless of their specific implementation. The .NET framework defines several collection interfaces, such as IEnumerable, ICollection, and IList, that define a set of common methods and properties that collections should implement.

Here's an overview of some of the most commonly used collection interfaces:

IEnumerable: The IEnumerable interface provides a way to iterate over a collection using a foreach loop. It defines a single method, GetEnumerator(), that returns an enumerator object that can be used to iterate over the collection.

```
47
48    public interface IEnumerable
49    {
50        IEnumerator GetEnumerator();
51    }
52
```

ICollection: The ICollection interface extends IEnumerable and adds methods for adding, removing, and checking the presence of elements in a collection.

```
53
54    public interface ICollection<T> : IEnumerable<T>
55    {
56        int Count { get; }
57        bool IsReadOnly { get; }
58        void Add(T item);
59        void Clear();
60        bool Contains(T item);
61        void CopyTo(T[] array, int arrayIndex);
62        bool Remove(T item);
63    }
64
65
```

IList: The IList interface extends ICollection and provides methods for inserting, removing, and accessing elements at a specific position in the collection.

```
65
66    public interface IList<T> : ICollection<T>, IEnumerable<T>
67    {
68        T this[int index] { get; set; }
69        int IndexOf(T item);
70        void Insert(int index, T item);
71        void RemoveAt(int index);
72    }
73
```

By using collection interfaces in your code, you can write more generic and reusable code that works with different types of collections. For example, you can create a method that takes an IEnumerable parameter, and use it to work with any collection that implements the IEnumerable interface. This can make your code more flexible and easier to maintain.

6

Exception handling

Exception handling is an important feature of C# that allows you to handle and recover from errors that occur during program execution. In C#, exceptions are represented by objects of the Exception class (or one of its derived classes). When an error occurs, an exception object is created and thrown, which causes the program execution to stop and transfer control to the nearest exception handler.

Here's a brief summary of the key concepts related to exception handling in C#:

- Throwing exceptions: You can throw an exception in your code using the throw statement. This causes the program execution to stop and transfer control to the nearest exception handler.
- Catching exceptions: You can catch an exception in your code using the try-catch statement. This allows you to handle the exception and take appropriate action, such as logging the error or displaying a message to the user.
- Handling specific exceptions: You can catch specific types of exceptions by specifying the exception type in the catch block. This allows you to handle different types of errors in different ways.
- Using finally blocks: You can use a finally block to specify code that should always be executed, regardless of whether an exception was thrown or not.

EXCEPTION HANDLING

This is useful for releasing resources or cleaning up after an operation.

- Raising exceptions: You can define your own exception classes by deriving from the Exception class, and throw instances of your custom exception classes when errors occur in your code. This allows you to create more meaningful and specific error messages for your users.

In summary, exception handling is a powerful feature of C# that allows you to handle and recover from errors that occur during program execution. By using the try-catch statement, you can catch and handle exceptions, and take appropriate action to recover from errors and prevent program crashes. By defining your own exception classes, you can create more meaningful and specific error messages for your users.

Throwing and catching exceptions

In C#, you can use the **throw** keyword to explicitly throw an exception when an error occurs during program execution. For example, you can throw a **DivideByZeroException** when dividing by zero:

```
int x = 10;
int y = 0;
if (y == 0)
{
    throw new DivideByZeroException();
}
int z = x / y; // This line will not be executed
```

In this example, if **y** is equal to zero, a **DivideByZeroException** is thrown. The program execution stops and control is transferred to the nearest **catch** block that can handle the exception.

When you throw an exception, you can provide an optional error message that describes the reason for the exception:

```
10
11    throw new Exception("Something went wrong");
12
```

By catching and handling exceptions, you can recover from errors and take appropriate action, such as displaying an error message or logging the error for debugging purposes.

When an exception is thrown, the program execution stops and control is transferred to the nearest catch block that can handle the exception. The catch block takes an exception parameter that represents the exception that was thrown. You can use the exception parameter to get information about the error that occurred, such as the error message or the stack trace.

You can also use multiple catch blocks to handle different types of exceptions. Here's an example:

```
14    try
15    {
16        // some code that may throw an exception
17    }
18    catch (FormatException ex)
19    {
20        // handle FormatException
21    }
22    catch (DivideByZeroException ex)
23    {
24        // handle DivideByZeroException
25    }
26    catch (Exception ex)
27    {
28        // handle any other type of exception
29    }
30
```

In this example, the first catch block handles a FormatException, the second catch block handles a DivideByZeroException, and the third catch block handles any other type of exception that was not caught by the previous catch blocks.

It's important to handle exceptions in your code to prevent program crashes and provide a better user experience. By catching and handling exceptions, you can recover from errors and take appropriate action, such as displaying an error message or logging the error for debugging purposes.

Handling specific exceptions

In C#, you can use **catch** blocks to handle specific exceptions that may be thrown in your code. This allows you to write specific code to handle different types of exceptions.

For example, consider the following code that attempts to read a file:

```
32
33    try
34    {
35        string filePath = "example.txt";
36        string fileContents = File.ReadAllText(filePath);
37        Console.WriteLine(fileContents);
38    }
39    catch (FileNotFoundException ex)
40    {
41        Console.WriteLine("File not found: " + ex.FileName);
42    }
43    catch (IOException ex)
44    {
45        Console.WriteLine("Error reading file: " + ex.Message);
46    }
47    catch (Exception ex)
48    {
49        Console.WriteLine("An error occurred: " + ex.Message);
50    }
51
```

In this example, the **try** block attempts to read the contents of a file specified by **filePath**. If the file is not found, a **FileNotFoundException** is thrown. If an I/O error occurs while reading the file, an **IOException** is thrown. Any other exceptions are caught by the final **catch** block, which simply prints a generic error message.

By catching specific exceptions, you can handle them in a more meaningful way than simply catching all exceptions. This allows you to provide more useful error messages and take appropriate action based on the specific error that occurred.

Using finally blocks

In C#, you can use a **finally** block to ensure that certain code is executed regardless of whether an exception is thrown or not. The code in the **finally** block is executed after the **try** block and any associated **catch** blocks have completed.

Here's an example of how to use a **finally** block:

```
FileStream fileStream = null;
try
{
    fileStream = new FileStream("example.txt", FileMode.Open);
    // Read from the file stream here
}
catch (IOException ex)
{
    Console.WriteLine("An error occurred: " + ex.Message);
}
finally
{
    if (fileStream != null)
    {
        fileStream.Close();
    }
}
```

In this example, a **FileStream** is opened in a **try** block for reading from the file "example.txt". If an **IOException** occurs while reading from the file, the error is caught in a **catch** block, and an error message is printed. Regardless of whether an exception is thrown or not, the **finally** block ensures that the file stream is closed when the code execution leaves the **try** block.

Using a **finally** block is useful for releasing resources, such as file handles or database connections, which should be closed regardless of whether an exception occurs or not.

7

File I/O

File I/O, or input/output, is the process of reading and writing data to and from files on disk. In C#, you can perform file I/O using the **System.IO** namespace, which provides classes for working with files and directories.

To read from a file, you can use the **File.ReadAllText()** method, which reads the entire contents of a file into a string. Alternatively, you can use the **FileStream** class to read from a file one byte at a time, or in larger chunks using a buffer.

To write to a file, you can use the **File.WriteAllText()** method, which writes a string to a file. You can also use the **FileStream** class to write to a file one byte at a time, or in larger chunks using a buffer.

In addition to reading and writing files, the **System.IO** namespace provides methods for working with directories and paths. You can create, delete, and move directories using the **Directory** class, and you can manipulate file paths using the **Path** class.

File I/O can be error-prone, so it's important to use exception handling to handle potential errors. For example, if a file is not found or cannot be opened, a **FileNotFoundException** or **IOException** may be thrown. You can use **try/catch** blocks to catch these exceptions and handle them appropriately.

Reading and writing text files

In C#, you can read and write text files using the **System.IO** namespace. Here's an example of how to read the contents of a text file:

```
3
4    string filePath = "path/to/file.txt";
5    string content = File.ReadAllText(filePath);
6    Console.WriteLine(content);
7
```

In this example, the **File.ReadAllText()** method is used to read the entire contents of the file at the specified path into a string. The **Console.WriteLine()** method is then used to output the contents of the file to the console.

To write to a text file, you can use the **File.WriteAllText()** method, like this:

```
7
8    string filePath = "path/to/file.txt";
9    string content = "This is some text that will be written to the file.";
10   File.WriteAllText(filePath, content);
11
12
```

In this example, the **File.WriteAllText()** method is used to write the specified string to the file at the specified path. If the file does not exist, it will be created. If it does exist, its contents will be overwritten.

It's important to remember to close the file after reading from or writing to it, to ensure that any resources associated with the file are released. To do this, you can use a **using** statement, like this:

```
12
13   string filePath = "path/to/file.txt";
14   using (FileStream fileStream = File.Open(filePath, FileMode.Open))
15   {
16       // Read from or write to the file here
17   }
18
```

In this example, a **FileStream** is created using the **File.Open()** method, which opens the file at the specified path in read/write mode. The **using** statement ensures that the **FileStream** is automatically closed when the code inside the block is finished executing.

Reading and writing binary files

In addition to reading and writing text files, you can also read and write binary files in C#. Binary files are files that contain data in a binary format, rather than as plain text.

To read from a binary file, you can use the **BinaryReader** class, which is part of the **System.IO** namespace. Here's an example:

```
19
20     string filePath = "path/to/file.bin";
21     using (FileStream fileStream = File.Open(filePath, FileMode.Open))
22     {
23         using (BinaryReader reader = new BinaryReader(fileStream))
24         {
25             int value1 = reader.ReadInt32();
26             double value2 = reader.ReadDouble();
27             string value3 = reader.ReadString();
28
29             Console.WriteLine("Value 1: " + value1);
30             Console.WriteLine("Value 2: " + value2);
31             Console.WriteLine("Value 3: " + value3);
32         }
33     }
34
```

In this example, a **FileStream** is opened in read mode and wrapped in a **BinaryReader**. The **BinaryReader** is then used to read an integer, a double, and a string from the file. The values are then output to the console.

To write to a binary file, you can use the **BinaryWriter** class, which is also part of the **System.IO** namespace. Here's an example:

```
35
36    string filePath = "path/to/file.bin";
37    using (FileStream fileStream = File.Open(filePath, FileMode.Create))
38    {
39        using (BinaryWriter writer = new BinaryWriter(fileStream))
40        {
41            int value1 = 42;
42            double value2 = 3.14159;
43            string value3 = "Hello, world!";
44
45            writer.Write(value1);
46            writer.Write(value2);
47            writer.Write(value3);
48        }
49    }
```

In this example, a **FileStream** is opened in write mode and wrapped in a **BinaryWriter**. The **BinaryWriter** is then used to write an integer, a double, and a string to the file.

It's important to remember that binary files may contain data in a specific format, such as little-endian or big-endian, and that this format may affect how the data is read or written. Additionally, binary files may contain data that is not human-readable, so it's important to be careful when working with them.

Working with directories and paths

In addition to reading and writing files, you may also need to work with directories and file paths in your C# programs. The **System.IO** namespace provides several classes and methods for working with directories and paths.

Here are some common tasks that you may need to perform when working with directories and paths in C#:

Creating a Directory

To create a new directory, you can use the **Directory.CreateDirectory()** method. Here's an example:

```
53    string path = @"C:\Users\JohnDoe\Documents\NewDirectory";
54
55    if (!Directory.Exists(path))
56    {
57        Directory.CreateDirectory(path);
58    }
```

In this example, the **Directory.CreateDirectory()** method is used to create a new directory at the specified path, if the directory does not already exist.

Listing Files in a Directory

To list the files in a directory, you can use the **Directory.GetFiles()** method. Here's an example:

```
60    string path = @"C:\Users\JohnDoe\Documents";
61
62    string[] files = Directory.GetFiles(path);
63
64    foreach (string file in files)
65    {
66        Console.WriteLine(file);
67    }
68
```

In this example, the **Directory.GetFiles()** method is used to get an array of file paths in the specified directory. The **foreach** loop is then used to iterate over the array and print each file path to the console.

Getting the Current Directory

To get the current working directory of your application, you can use the **Directory.GetCurrentDirectory()** method. Here's an example:

```
69
70    string currentDirectory = Directory.GetCurrentDirectory();
71
72    Console.WriteLine(currentDirectory);
73
```

In this example, the **Directory.GetCurrentDirectory()** method is used to get the current working directory of the application, which is then printed to the console.

Getting the Parent Directory

To get the parent directory of a file or directory, you can use the **Path.GetDirectoryName()** method. Here's an example:

```
69
70    string currentDirectory = Directory.GetCurrentDirectory();
71
72    Console.WriteLine(currentDirectory);
73
74
75    string path = @"C:\Users\JohnDoe\Documents\MyFile.txt";
76
77    string parentDirectory = Path.GetDirectoryName(path);
78
79    Console.WriteLine(parentDirectory);
80
```

In this example, the **Path.GetDirectoryName()** method is used to get the parent directory of the specified file path, which is then printed to the console.

Combining Paths

To combine two or more paths into a single path, you can use the **Path.Combine()** method. Here's an example:

```
81
82    string directory = @"C:\Users\JohnDoe\Documents";
83    string filename = "MyFile.txt";
84
85    string fullPath = Path.Combine(directory, filename);
86
87    Console.WriteLine(fullPath);
88
```

In this example, the **Path.Combine()** method is used to combine the directory path and the filename into a single full path, which is then printed to the console.

Working with directories and paths is an important part of many C# applications. By using the classes and methods provided by the **System.IO** namespace, you can easily perform common tasks such as creating directories, listing files, and combining paths.

8

Regular Expressions

Regular expressions are a powerful tool for working with text data in C#. They provide a way to search for and manipulate text patterns based on specific rules or patterns. Regular expressions in C# are represented by the System.Text.RegularExpressions namespace, which provides a set of classes and methods for working with regular expressions.

In C#, regular expressions can be used to perform a variety of text processing tasks, such as validating input, searching for specific patterns or substrings, and replacing text. Regular expressions are made up of a combination of literal characters and special characters that represent certain patterns or rules.

The System.Text.RegularExpressions namespace provides several classes and methods for working with regular expressions in C#. These include the Regex class, which provides methods for compiling and executing regular expressions, and the Match and Group classes, which provide information about the results of a regular expression search.

To use regular expressions in C#, you typically create a Regex object, compile the regular expression pattern, and then use the Match and Group classes to search for and extract the desired text.

Regular expressions can be a powerful tool for text processing in C#, but they can also be complex and difficult to understand. It is important to carefully test and validate regular expressions before using them in production code.

Understanding regular expressions

Regular expressions are a pattern matching language used to search and manipulate text based on specific rules or patterns. In C#, regular expressions are represented by the System.Text.RegularExpressions namespace, which provides a set of classes and methods for working with regular expressions.

A regular expression is made up of a combination of literal characters and special characters that represent certain patterns or rules. For example, the regular expression pattern "hello" would match any string that contains the letters "hello" in sequence.

Literal characters and metacharacters

In regular expressions, literal characters are any characters that match themselves, such as letters, digits, and punctuation marks. For example, the regular expression pattern "cat" would match the characters "cat" in a string.

Metacharacters, on the other hand, have special meanings in regular expressions and are used to represent certain patterns or rules. Some common metacharacters include:

- "." – matches any single character except a newline character
- "*" – matches zero or more of the preceding character or group
- "+" – matches one or more of the preceding character or group
- "?" – matches zero or one of the preceding character or group
- "^" – matches the beginning of a line or string
- "$" – matches the end of a line or string
- "[" and "]" – creates a character set, matches any one of the characters within the brackets
- "(" and ")" – groups characters together for use with other special characters
- "|" – matches either the preceding or following character or group

87

By combining literal characters and metacharacters in a regular expression pattern, you can create complex search and match criteria for text processing tasks in C#. It is important to carefully test and validate regular expressions before using them in production code, as incorrect or incomplete regular expressions can result in unexpected behavior or security vulnerabilities.

Character classes and quantifiers

In addition to literal characters and metacharacters, regular expressions in C# also use character classes and quantifiers.

Character classes are enclosed in square brackets and represent a set of characters that can be matched by a single character in the input string. For example, the character class "[aeiou]" matches any vowel character. You can also use character ranges in character classes, such as "[a-z]" to match any lowercase letter.

Quantifiers are used to specify the number of times a character or character class should be matched. Some common quantifiers include:

- "*" - matches zero or more occurrences
- "+" - matches one or more occurrences
- "?" - matches zero or one occurrence
- "{n}" - matches exactly n occurrences
- "{n,}" - matches n or more occurrences
- "{n,m}" - matches between n and m occurrences

For example, the regular expression pattern "a{2,4}" would match any string containing between 2 and 4 consecutive "a" characters.

By combining literal characters, metacharacters, character classes, and quantifiers in various ways, you can create complex regular expression patterns that can match and extract specific patterns of text from input strings in C#. Regular expressions are a powerful tool for text processing, but it's important to use them carefully and validate them thoroughly to avoid unintended consequences or security vulnerabilities.

Grouping and capturing

Grouping and capturing are advanced features of regular expressions in C# that allow you to match and extract specific portions of a pattern from an input string.

Grouping is used to apply a quantifier to a group of characters or metacharacters. To create a group, you enclose a pattern in parentheses. For example, the regular expression pattern "a(bc)*" matches any string containing the substring "abc" zero or more times.

Capturing is used to extract the matched contents of a group from the input string. When a group is matched, the matched contents are stored in a capture group, which can be accessed using the Groups property of the Match object returned by the Regex.Match method. For example, the regular expression "(?<day>\d{2})/(?<month>\d{2})/(?<year>\d{4})" matches a date string in the format "dd/mm/yyyy" and captures the day, month, and year values as named capture groups.

C# also provides a shorthand syntax for named capture groups, using the syntax "(?P<name>pattern)" to define a named capture group. For example, the regular expression "(?P<day>\d{2})/(?P<month>\d{2})/(?P<year>\d{4})" is equivalent to the previous example, but uses the shorthand syntax for named capture groups.

By using grouping and capturing in regular expressions, you can create powerful search and replace operations, data validation and transformation operations, and more. However, it's important to understand the syntax and behavior of regular expressions in C# to avoid unintended consequences or security vulnerabilities.

Lookarounds and backreferences

Lookarounds and backreferences are two advanced features of regular expressions in C# that allow you to perform more complex pattern matching and substitution operations.

Lookarounds are zero-width assertions that allow you to match a pattern only if it is preceded or followed by another pattern. There are two types of lookarounds: positive lookarounds and negative lookarounds. Positive lookarounds are written as "(?=pattern)" and match the pattern only if it is followed by the lookahead pattern. Negative lookarounds are written as "(?!pattern)" and match the pattern only if it is not followed by the lookahead pattern.

Backreferences allow you to refer to a captured group within the same regular expression pattern. To create a backreference, you use the syntax "\n", where "n" is the index of the capture group you want to reference. For example, the regular expression pattern "(\w)\1" matches any string containing a repeated character, such as "hello" or "bookkeeper".

In addition to lookarounds and backreferences, C# also provides a range of other advanced features for regular expressions, including named capture groups, non-capturing groups, conditional expressions, and more. These features allow you to create more powerful and flexible regular expressions for a wide range of applications, from text processing and data validation to search and replace operations and more.

However, it's important to use these advanced features with care and to thoroughly test your regular expressions to ensure that they are accurate and efficient. Regular expressions can be powerful tools, but they can also be complex and difficult to debug if used incorrectly.

Using regular expressions in C#

In C#, regular expressions can be used to perform pattern matching and substitution operations on strings. The .NET Framework includes a regular expression engine that supports a wide range of regular expression syntax and features.

To use regular expressions in C#, you first need to create a regular expression pattern. This pattern is a string that defines the pattern you want to match or replace. For example, the pattern "\b[A-Z0-9._%+-]+@[A-Z0-9.-]+.[A-Z]{2,}\b" matches email addresses in a string.

Once you have created a regular expression pattern, you can use the Regex class in C# to apply the pattern to a string. The Regex class provides a range of methods for performing regular expression operations, including methods for matching, replacing, and splitting strings based on regular expression patterns.

Here is an example of using regular expressions in C# to match email addresses in a string:

```
string input = "Please contact us at support@example.com for assistance.";
string pattern = @"\b[A-Z0-9._%+-]+@[A-Z0-9.-]+\.[A-Z]{2,}\b";
Regex regex = new Regex(pattern, RegexOptions.IgnoreCase);
MatchCollection matches = regex.Matches(input);
foreach (Match match in matches)
{
    Console.WriteLine("Email address found: {0}", match.Value);
}
```

In this example, we create a regular expression pattern that matches email addresses, using the "\b" anchor to match word boundaries, character classes to match specific characters and ranges of characters, and quantifiers to match one or more occurrences of a pattern. We then create a Regex object with the pattern and RegexOptions.IgnoreCase to perform case-insensitive matching. We use the Matches method to find all the email addresses in the input string, and then use a foreach loop to print out each match.

Regular expressions can be a powerful tool for text processing in C#, but they can also be complex and difficult to understand. It's important to carefully test your regular expressions and to use them with care, especially when dealing with user input or sensitive data.

Creating regular expression patterns with the Regex class

The Regex class in C# provides a powerful and efficient way to work with regular expressions. Here are the basic steps for using regular expressions with the Regex class:

1. Create a regular expression pattern using a string that contains the

pattern you want to match.

2. Create an instance of the Regex class by passing the regular expression pattern as a parameter to the constructor.

3. Call the appropriate method on the Regex instance to match the pattern against the input string. The most common method is Match, which returns a Match object that provides information about the first match found in the input string.

4. Use the properties and methods of the Match object to retrieve information about the match, such as the matched text and the position of the match in the input string.

5. Repeat steps 3 and 4 as needed to find additional matches in the input string.

Here's an example that demonstrates how to use the Regex class to match a regular expression pattern:

```
13
14   using System;
15   using System.Text.RegularExpressions;
16
17   class Program
18   {
19       static void Main()
20       {
21           string input = "The quick brown fox jumps over the lazy dog";
22           string pattern = "\\b[a-z]{4}\\b";
23
24           Regex regex = new Regex(pattern);
25           Match match = regex.Match(input);
26
27           if (match.Success)
28           {
29               Console.WriteLine("Match found at position {0}: {1}",
30                   match.Index, match.Value);
31           }
32           else
33           {
34               Console.WriteLine("No match found.");
35           }
36       }
37   }
```

In this example, we create a regular expression pattern that matches any four-letter word in the input string. We then create a Regex instance with the pattern and call the Match method to find the first match in the input string. If a match is found, we output the position of the match and the matched text. Otherwise, we output a message indicating that no match was found.

The Regex class in C# also provides a number of other methods and options for working with regular expressions, such as Replace for replacing matched text, Split for splitting a string into substrings based on a regular expression pattern, and various options for controlling the behavior of the regular expression engine.

Using regular expressions for pattern matching

In C#, you can use regular expressions for pattern matching using the **Regex** class. The **Regex** class provides a powerful set of methods for working with regular expressions, including:

- **Match**: Searches the input string for the first occurrence of a regular expression match.
- **Matches**: Searches the input string for all occurrences of a regular expression match.
- **Replace**: Replaces all occurrences of a regular expression match in the input string with a replacement string.
- **Split**: Splits the input string into an array of substrings based on a regular expression match.

To use regular expressions for pattern matching in C#, you first need to create a **Regex** object by compiling a regular expression pattern. For example, to match a string that starts with "Hello" and ends with "world!", you could create a **Regex** object as follows:

```
38
39    Regex regex = new Regex("^Hello.*world!$");
```

Once you have a **Regex** object, you can use its methods to perform pattern matching on input strings. For example, to check if a string matches the pattern, you could use the **IsMatch** method:

```
39   Regex regex = new Regex("^Hello.*world!$");
40
41
42   string input = "Hello, world!";
43   if (regex.IsMatch(input))
44   {
45       Console.WriteLine("Match found!");
46   }
47   else
48   {
49       Console.WriteLine("No match found.");
50   }
51
```

You can also use regular expression groups to extract specific parts of the input string that match a pattern. For example, to extract a phone number from a string that contains both the phone number and the person's name, you could use a regular expression pattern with a group:

```
53   string input = "John Smith: 555-1234";
54   Regex regex = new Regex(@"(\d{3})-(\d{4})");
55   Match match = regex.Match(input);
56   if (match.Success)
57   {
58       string phoneNumber = match.Groups[1].Value + "-" + match.Groups[2].Value;
59       Console.WriteLine("Phone number: " + phoneNumber);
60   }
61   else
62   {
63       Console.WriteLine("No phone number found.");
64   }
```

In this example, the regular expression pattern **(\d{3})-(\d{4})** matches a phone number in the format "555-1234" and uses two groups to capture the three-digit area code and the four-digit phone number. The **Match** method searches the input string for a match to this pattern, and the **Groups** property of the resulting **Match** object contains the captured groups.

Extracting matches and groups

In C#, you can extract matches and groups from a string using regular expressions and the **Regex** class.

To extract matches, you first need to create a regular expression pattern that matches the desired string or pattern. You then use the **Match** method of the **Regex** class to find all matches in the input string. The **Match** method returns a **MatchCollection** object that contains all the matches.

Here's an example that extracts all email addresses from a string:

```
using System;
using System.Text.RegularExpressions;

class Program
{
    static void Main()
    {
        string input = "Please contact us at support@example.com
                         or sales@example.com.";
        string pattern = @"\w+@\w+\.\w+";
        Regex regex = new Regex(pattern);
        MatchCollection matches = regex.Matches(input);
        foreach (Match match in matches)
        {
            Console.WriteLine(match.Value);
        }
    }
}
```

In this example, the regular expression pattern **\w+@\w+\.\w+** matches any email address in the input string. The **Match** method finds all matches of this pattern in the input string, and the **foreach** loop prints each match to the console.

To extract groups from a match, you can use the **Groups** property of the **Match** object. The **Groups** property returns a collection of groups, where group 0 represents the entire match and subsequent groups represent any capturing groups in the pattern.

Here's an example that extracts the username and domain name from an email address:

```
86
87    using System;
88    using System.Text.RegularExpressions;
89
90    class Program
91    {
92        static void Main()
93        {
94            string input = "support@example.com";
95            string pattern = @"(\w+)@(\w+)\.(\w+)";
96            Regex regex = new Regex(pattern);
97            Match match = regex.Match(input);
98            if (match.Success)
99            {
100               Console.WriteLine("Username: " + match.Groups[1].Value);
101               Console.WriteLine("Domain: " + match.Groups[2].Value);
102               Console.WriteLine("TLD: " + match.Groups[3].Value);
103           }
104       }
105   }
```

In this example, the regular expression pattern **(\w+)@(\w+)\.(\w+)** matches an email address and captures the username, domain name, and top-level domain (TLD) in three separate groups. The **Match** method finds the first match of this pattern in the input string, and the **if** statement checks if the match was successful. The **Groups** property of the **Match** object is used to extract the captured groups, which are then printed to the console.

In summary, you can extract matches and groups from a string in C# using regular expressions and the **Regex** class. The **Match** method finds all matches of a given pattern in the input string and returns a **MatchCollection** object. The **Groups** property of the **Match** object is used to extract the captured groups in a match.

Replacing text with regular expressions

In C#, you can use regular expressions to search for and replace text in a string or file. The Regex class provides methods for replacing text using regular expressions.

The basic syntax for replacing text using regular expressions is:

```
106
107    Regex.Replace(input, pattern, replacement);
108
```

Here, **input** is the string or file that you want to search and replace, **pattern** is the regular expression pattern that you want to search for, and **replacement** is the replacement string that you want to use.

For example, the following code replaces all occurrences of the word "fox" with "dog" in a string:

```
107    Regex.Replace(input, pattern, replacement);
108
109    string input = "The quick brown fox jumps over the lazy dog.";
110    string pattern = "fox";
111    string replacement = "dog";
112    string result = Regex.Replace(input, pattern, replacement);
113    Console.WriteLine(result);
```

The output of this code is:

```
114
115    The quick brown dog jumps over the lazy dog.
```

You can also use regular expression groups to create more complex replacement patterns. For example, the following code replaces all occurrences of a date in the format "MM/DD/YYYY" with a date in the format "YYYY-MM-DD":

```
116
117    string input = "Today is 10/31/2022.";
118    string pattern = @"(\d{2})/(\d{2})/(\d{4})";
119    string replacement = @"$3-$1-$2";
120    string result = Regex.Replace(input, pattern, replacement);
121    Console.WriteLine(result);
122
```

The output of this code is:

```
122
123      Today is 2022-10-31.
```

In this example, the regular expression pattern @"(\d{2})/(\d{2})/(\d{4})" matches a date in the format "MM/DD/YYYY" and captures the month, day, and year as three separate groups. The replacement string @"$3-$1-$2" uses these groups to create a new date in the format "YYYY-MM-DD".

Best practices for regular expressions

Best practices for regular expressions in C# include:

- Use regular expressions only when necessary: Regular expressions can be powerful, but they can also be slow and hard to read. Use them only when necessary and consider other options like string methods or LINQ.
- Use descriptive variable names: When using regular expressions, use variable names that describe what the regular expression is doing. This makes the code more readable and easier to understand.
- Test regular expressions thoroughly: Test regular expressions with a variety of inputs, including edge cases and invalid inputs, to make sure they work correctly.
- Use RegexOptions to modify regular expression behavior: RegexOptions can be used to modify regular expression behavior, such as ignoring case or allowing whitespace. Use them when necessary to make regular expressions more flexible.
- Break complex regular expressions into smaller parts: If a regular expression is too complex, consider breaking it into smaller parts or using multiple regular expressions to accomplish the task.
- Comment regular expressions: Use comments to explain what a regular expression is doing and why it is necessary. This makes the code easier to understand and maintain.
- Use tools to help with regular expressions: There are many tools available

that can help with creating, testing, and debugging regular expressions. Use them to make regular expressions easier to work with.

Optimizing regular expressions for performance

When working with regular expressions in C#, there are several best practices you can follow to optimize performance:

- Use the most specific pattern possible: Regular expressions can be computationally expensive, so it's best to use the most specific pattern possible to match your desired text. This will reduce the amount of backtracking required by the regex engine.
- Use compiled regular expressions: In C#, you can use the **Regex.Compile** method to pre-compile a regular expression pattern for faster execution. This can be particularly useful if you need to use the same pattern multiple times.
- Use lazy quantifiers: Lazy quantifiers, denoted by the **?** character, are less greedy than their greedy counterparts and can reduce the amount of backtracking required by the regex engine. For example, **.*?** will match the smallest possible string, while **.*** will match the largest possible string.
- Use character classes instead of alternations: When matching a single character from a set of alternatives, it's generally more efficient to use a character class, denoted by square brackets, than an alternation, denoted by the | character. For example, **[aeiou]** will match any vowel, while **a|e|i|o|u** will also match any vowel but is less efficient.
- Avoid unnecessary capturing groups: Capturing groups, denoted by parentheses, can be useful for extracting information from a matched string. However, unnecessary capturing groups can slow down the regex engine, so it's best to use them sparingly.

By following these best practices, you can improve the performance of your regular expressions in C# and ensure that they run efficiently, even on large input strings.

Testing regular expressions with test tools

Testing regular expressions is an essential part of developing robust applications that rely on them. It can help to catch syntax errors, ensure that the pattern matches the desired strings, and improve the performance of the pattern.

There are several tools available that can help you test regular expressions, including:

- RegexStorm.net: A free online tool that allows you to test regular expressions in real-time, highlighting matches in your input text.
- RegExr: A free online tool that allows you to build, test, and debug regular expressions, with a visual representation of the matches.
- Expresso: A commercial tool that provides a comprehensive testing environment for regular expressions, including syntax highlighting, debugging, and a library of pre-built patterns.
- RegexBuddy: Another commercial tool that provides a powerful testing environment for regular expressions, with a comprehensive library of pre-built patterns, syntax highlighting, and debugging.

When testing regular expressions, it's essential to use representative input data that includes a range of edge cases, such as empty strings, null values, and special characters. You should also test the pattern's performance with large data sets to ensure that it doesn't impact application performance.

In summary, testing regular expressions is an essential part of developing robust applications that rely on them. There are several tools available that can help you test regular expressions, and it's important to use representative input data and test for performance with large data sets.

Understanding common regular expression pitfalls and mistakes

Regular expressions can be a powerful tool for working with text, but they can also be tricky to use correctly. Here are some common pitfalls and mistakes to watch out for:

- Greedy quantifiers: By default, regular expression quantifiers such as *****
  and **+** are greedy, meaning they will match as much text as possible. This
  can lead to unexpected matches and performance issues, especially when
  dealing with large amounts of data. To avoid this, use lazy quantifiers (***?**
  and **+?**) or use character classes to be more specific about what should be
  matched.
- Incorrect character escaping: Regular expressions use certain characters
  to denote metacharacters, such as . to match any character and ∧ to match
  the start of a line. If you want to match these characters literally, you
  need to escape them with a backslash (\). However, if you forget to escape
  them, you may get unexpected matches or errors.
- Not using anchors correctly: Regular expression anchors (∧ and **$**) are
  used to match the start and end of a line, respectively. If you forget to use
  these anchors, your regular expression may match text in the middle of a
  line, leading to unexpected matches.
- Overcomplicating regular expressions: Regular expressions can quickly
  become very complex, making them hard to read, understand, and
  maintain. Try to keep your regular expressions as simple as possible
  and use comments to explain what each part of the expression is doing.
- Not testing regular expressions thoroughly: Regular expressions can be
  tricky to get right, so it's important to test them thoroughly before using
  them in production. Use test tools such as RegExr or Regex101 to test your
  regular expressions with different inputs and edge cases.

By avoiding these common pitfalls and mistakes, you can use regular expressions more effectively and avoid unexpected results or errors.

9

Debugging and Testing

Debugging and testing are important aspects of software development. Debugging is the process of finding and fixing errors in code, while testing is the process of evaluating the functionality of software.

In C#, debugging can be done using the debugger tool in Visual Studio, which allows developers to step through code and examine variables and memory. Unit testing can be done using a testing framework like NUnit, which provides tools for defining and running tests, and evaluating the results.

Test-driven development (TDD) is an approach to software development that emphasizes writing tests before writing code. In TDD, tests are written for a specific feature before the feature is implemented. This approach helps ensure that the code meets the requirements and reduces the likelihood of introducing bugs.

Best practices for debugging and testing in C# include using meaningful variable names, avoiding hardcoded values, using automated testing frameworks, and testing edge cases.

In summary, debugging and testing are critical components of software development, and C# provides tools like the debugger and NUnit for these tasks. TDD is an approach that emphasizes writing tests before writing code, and best practices include using meaningful variable names, avoiding hardcoded values, and testing edge cases.

Using the debugger

Using the debugger is an essential skill for every developer, and it is an efficient way to debug and diagnose issues in code. In C#, you can use the built-in debugger in Visual Studio or other IDEs to step through code, inspect variables, and set breakpoints to stop execution at specific points.

The debugger provides many useful features such as:

- Stepping through code line by line
- Setting breakpoints to pause execution at a specific point
- Inspecting the value of variables at runtime
- Evaluating expressions and watching variables
- Debugging multi-threaded applications
- Debugging remote applications

By using the debugger effectively, you can quickly find and fix bugs in your code, improving the quality and reliability of your software.

Setting breakpoints and stepping through code

Setting breakpoints and stepping through code are fundamental features of debugging in C#. Setting breakpoints allows you to stop the execution of your program at a specific line of code, and step through code allows you to execute your program one line at a time.

To set a breakpoint, simply click on the left-hand margin of the code editor at the line where you want to stop execution. When your program runs, it will stop at the breakpoint, and you can then use the debugger to examine the current state of the program, including the values of variables and the call stack.

Once you have stopped at a breakpoint, you can use the step commands to execute your program one line at a time. The most common step commands are:

- Step Over (F10): Executes the current line of code and moves to the next line.
- Step Into (F11): Executes the current line of code, and if it is a method call, it steps into the method and stops at the first line of the method.
- Step Out (Shift + F11): Continues execution of the program until the current method returns.

Using the debugger is an essential tool for finding and fixing bugs in your code. By setting breakpoints and stepping through code, you can quickly identify where the problem lies and fix it.

In summary, setting breakpoints and stepping through code are fundamental features of debugging in C#. By using the debugger to examine the current state of your program, you can quickly identify bugs and fix them.

Inspecting variables and objects

When using a debugger in C#, you can inspect the values of variables and objects at various points in the code. This can help you identify the source of errors and understand how the program is working. Here are some ways to inspect variables and objects:

- Hovering over a variable or object: You can hover over a variable or object in the code editor while the program is running to see its current value.
- Using the Locals and Autos windows: The Locals window shows the values of local variables in the current scope, while the Autos window shows the values of variables related to the current line of code.
- Using the Watch window: The Watch window allows you to specify variables or expressions to monitor as the program runs. You can add variables to the Watch window by right-clicking on them in the code editor and selecting "Add to Watch".
- Using the Immediate window: The Immediate window allows you to execute code and evaluate expressions in real-time as the program runs. You can use it to test code snippets and view the values of variables.

By inspecting variables and objects in these ways, you can gain a deeper understanding of how your program is working and quickly identify and fix errors.

Using the Immediate window and watch windows

In C#, the Immediate window and Watch windows are used during debugging to inspect variables and objects in real-time.

The Immediate window allows developers to execute code and evaluate expressions during debugging. It provides a command-line interface that can be used to execute statements and display their results. This window can be useful for quickly testing code snippets, evaluating expressions, or modifying variables on the fly.

The Watch windows allow developers to monitor the value of a specific variable or expression during debugging. It enables developers to add variables and expressions to a watch list and track their values as they change during program execution.

Both the Immediate and Watch windows can be useful for debugging complex code, identifying errors, and gaining a better understanding of how the code works. By using these tools, developers can quickly locate issues and gain insights into the behavior of the code at runtime.

Handling exceptions and errors

Handling exceptions and errors is a critical aspect of debugging and testing in C#. Exceptions and errors can occur when unexpected or invalid conditions arise during program execution, and they can cause a program to crash or behave unexpectedly. To handle exceptions and errors in C#, you can use several techniques:

- Try-catch blocks: A try-catch block allows you to catch exceptions that occur within a specific block of code and handle them in a graceful manner. The try block contains the code that might throw an exception, and the catch block contains the code that handles the exception.

- Finally blocks: A finally block is used to execute code that must always be executed, regardless of whether an exception is thrown or not. This block is typically used to release resources such as files or network connections that were acquired in the try block.
- Assertions: An assertion is a statement that tests a condition and throws an exception if the condition is not true. Assertions are useful for debugging and testing because they allow you to detect and diagnose problems in your code quickly.
- Logging: Logging is the process of recording information about a program's execution, such as error messages, warnings, and other events. By logging information, you can diagnose problems in your program and identify areas for improvement.
- Unit testing: Unit testing is the process of testing individual units of code, such as methods and functions, to ensure that they work correctly. Unit testing is typically automated and can be performed using tools such as NUnit.

In summary, handling exceptions and errors is an essential aspect of debugging and testing in C#. By using techniques such as try-catch blocks, finally blocks, assertions, logging, and unit testing, you can catch and handle exceptions and errors in a graceful manner, diagnose problems in your code, and ensure that your code works correctly.

Writing unit tests with NUnit

NUnit is a popular unit testing framework for C#. Writing unit tests is an essential part of software development to ensure that the code works as expected and to catch any bugs or errors early in the development process.

To use NUnit, you need to create a separate project in your solution dedicated to testing. In this project, you can create a test class and write test methods to test different parts of your code.

Each test method should use the Assert class to verify that the code under test behaves as expected. The Assert class provides a variety of methods to test for conditions such as equality, inequality, exceptions, and more.

Here's an example of a simple test method using NUnit:

```
[TestFixture]
public class MyTestClass
{
    [Test]
    public void TestMethod()
    {
        // Arrange
        int x = 5;
        int y = 10;

        // Act
        int result = x + y;

        // Assert
        Assert.AreEqual(15, result);
    }
}
```

In this example, the **[TestFixture]** attribute indicates that this class contains test methods, and the **[Test]** attribute indicates that this method is a test method. The **Arrange** section sets up the necessary variables and objects for the test. The **Act** section calls the method or code under test. The **Assert** section checks that the result of the method or code under test is what we expect it to be.

You can run your tests using the NUnit test runner, which can be integrated with Visual Studio or run from the command line. The test runner will show the results of each test method, including whether it passed or failed, and any error messages.

In summary, writing unit tests with NUnit is an important part of software development in C#. By creating a separate project for testing and writing test methods using the Assert class, you can ensure that your code works as expected and catch any bugs or errors early in the development process.

Introduction to unit testing

Unit testing is a software testing technique where individual units or components of a software application are tested in isolation from the rest of the system to ensure they behave as expected. The goal of unit testing is to verify the correctness and reliability of individual units of code.

In C#, unit testing is commonly performed using a unit testing framework such as NUnit, xUnit, or MSTest. These frameworks provide a set of tools and assertions to help developers write and run unit tests for their code.

Unit tests are typically written by developers as part of the software development process. A unit test typically consists of a set of inputs and an expected output. The test code executes the unit being tested with the inputs and compares the actual output with the expected output. If they match, the test passes; otherwise, it fails.

Unit testing has several benefits, including:

- Finding bugs early: By testing individual units of code in isolation, bugs can be detected and fixed earlier in the development process, when they are less expensive to fix.
- Refactoring: Unit tests can be used to ensure that changes to code do not introduce new bugs or break existing functionality.
- Documentation: Unit tests can serve as documentation for the behavior of the code.
- Quality assurance: Unit tests can improve the overall quality of the code by ensuring that it behaves as expected.

In summary, unit testing is a software testing technique where individual units or components of a software application are tested in isolation to ensure they behave as expected. Unit tests are typically written by developers and are commonly performed using a unit testing framework such as NUnit. Unit testing has several benefits, including finding bugs early, ensuring code changes do not introduce new bugs, serving as documentation, and improving overall code quality.

Creating test projects and test fixtures

When using NUnit for unit testing in C#, the first step is to create a new test project in your solution. This project should reference the NUnit framework, which can be installed using NuGet.

Once the test project is set up, you can create a test fixture class. A test fixture is a class that contains one or more test methods. Each test method should test a specific aspect of the code being tested.

Here's an example of a test fixture class:

```
using NUnit.Framework;

[TestFixture]
public class MyTests
{
    [Test]
    public void TestMethod1()
    {
        // Arrange
        int x = 2;
        int y = 3;

        // Act
        int result = x + y;

        // Assert
        Assert.AreEqual(5, result);
    }

    [Test]
    public void TestMethod2()
    {
        // Arrange
        string s = "hello world";

        // Act
        string result = s.ToUpper();

        // Assert
        Assert.AreEqual("HELLO WORLD", result);
    }
}
```

In this example, the **MyTests** class is marked with the **[TestFixture]** attribute to indicate that it is a test fixture. It contains two test methods: **TestMethod1** and **TestMethod2**. Each test method is marked with the **[Test]** attribute.

In the **TestMethod1** method, the Arrange step sets up two integer variables, **x** and **y**. The Act step adds these variables together and assigns the result to a new variable, **result**. The Assert step checks that **result** is equal to the expected value of 5.

In the **TestMethod2** method, the Arrange step sets up a string variable, **s**. The Act step converts this string to uppercase and assigns the result to a new variable, **result**. The Assert step checks that **result** is equal to the expected value of "HELLO WORLD".

By creating test fixture classes with multiple test methods, you can test different aspects of your code in a structured and repeatable way.

Writing test methods and assertions

In unit testing, a test method is a method that verifies that a specific piece of code behaves as expected. Test methods are typically written using a unit testing framework such as NUnit.

Here is an example of a simple test method in NUnit:

```
55
56    [Test]
57    public void TestAddition()
58    {
59        int result = Calculator.Add(2, 3);
60        Assert.AreEqual(5, result);
61    }
62
```

In this example, the **TestAddition** method is a test method that verifies that the **Add** method of the **Calculator** class returns the expected result when called with the arguments 2 and 3. The **Assert.AreEqual** method is used to compare the expected result (5) with the actual result returned by the **Add** method.

Unit tests typically follow a three-step process:

1. Arrange: Set up the necessary objects, data, and environment for the test.
2. Act: Invoke the method or code being tested.
3. Assert: Verify that the method or code being tested behaves as expected.

Here's an example of a more complex test method that follows this process:

```
63    [Test]
64    public void TestGetAllEmployees()
65    {
66        // Arrange
67        var employeeRepository = new EmployeeRepository();
68        employeeRepository.Add(new Employee("John", "Doe", 50000));
69        employeeRepository.Add(new Employee("Jane", "Smith", 60000));
70
71        // Act
72        var result = employeeRepository.GetAll();
73
74        // Assert
75        Assert.AreEqual(2, result.Count);
76        Assert.AreEqual("John", result[0].FirstName);
77        Assert.AreEqual("Doe", result[0].LastName);
78        Assert.AreEqual(50000, result[0].Salary);
79        Assert.AreEqual("Jane", result[1].FirstName);
80        Assert.AreEqual("Smith", result[1].LastName);
81        Assert.AreEqual(60000, result[1].Salary);
82    }
```

In this example, the **TestGetAllEmployees** method tests the **GetAll** method of the **EmployeeRepository** class, which is expected to return a list of all employees in the repository. The test sets up the repository with two employees, calls the **GetAll** method, and verifies that the result contains two employees with the expected properties.

In summary, a test method is a method that verifies that a specific piece of code behaves as expected. Test methods typically follow a three-step process of arranging the necessary objects and data, acting on the code being tested, and asserting that the code behaves as expected. Unit testing frameworks such as NUnit provide a framework for writing and running test methods.

Running and analyzing test results

After writing test methods, you can run them to check if your code is working as expected. In C#, you can use a testing framework like NUnit to create and run tests.

To run tests in NUnit, you need to create a test project and add the test fixtures and methods to it. Once you have written the tests, you can run them using the NUnit Test Runner.

The NUnit Test Runner provides a user interface for running and analyzing tests. When you run the tests, the Test Runner executes each test method and reports the results. You can see which tests passed, which failed, and any error messages that were generated.

You can also view detailed information about each test, including the test method name, the expected and actual values, and the time it took to run the test. This information can help you diagnose problems in your code and identify areas for improvement.

In addition to running tests manually, you can also automate the testing process using a continuous integration (CI) tool. A CI tool can automatically build and test your code every time you make changes, helping you catch errors and bugs early in the development process.

In summary, running and analyzing test results is an important part of the testing process in C#. You can use a testing framework like NUnit to create and run tests, and the NUnit Test Runner provides a user interface for executing and analyzing test results. By automating the testing process using a CI tool, you can catch errors and bugs early in the development process, improving the quality and reliability of your code.

Test-driven development (TDD)

Test-driven development (TDD) is a software development process that emphasizes writing automated tests before writing the code. In TDD, tests are used to define the requirements and specifications of the software, and the code is written to pass those tests.

The TDD process typically involves the following steps:

- Write a failing test: The developer writes a test that specifies the behavior of a new feature or function that they want to add to the software. This test should initially fail because the feature has not yet been implemented.
- Write the minimum code required to pass the test: The developer writes the minimum amount of code required to make the failing test pass. This code should not include any additional features or functionality beyond what is required to pass the test.
- Refactor the code: The developer refactors the code to improve its design and maintainability. This step ensures that the code is clean and follows best practices.
- Repeat the process: The developer repeats the process, adding more tests and functionality until the feature is complete.

The benefits of TDD include increased code quality, faster development cycles, and improved maintainability. TDD also helps to catch bugs early in the development process, when they are easier and cheaper to fix.

Writing tests before writing code

Writing tests before writing code is a fundamental concept of Test-Driven Development (TDD). It involves writing a test for a particular piece of functionality before actually writing the code that implements that functionality. The test is written to check that the code meets the requirements of the feature, and then the code is written to pass the test.

By following this process, developers can ensure that their code is tested thoroughly, and that they are only writing code that is necessary to pass the tests. This can lead to more maintainable and scalable code, as well as increased confidence in the code's correctness.

Refactoring and improving code based on tests

Refactoring and improving code based on tests is a crucial part of the Test-driven development (TDD) process. Once tests are written, they can be run to identify any failing tests. These failing tests help identify areas of the code that need improvement, refactoring, or debugging.

To improve code based on tests, developers can use the following steps:

- Analyze failing tests: Developers can analyze failing tests to understand why the tests are failing. They can use the error messages and stack traces to locate the source of the problem.
- Write code to fix failing tests: Developers can write code to fix the failing tests. They can use a debugger to step through the code and identify the cause of the problem. Once the problem is identified, developers can write code to fix the problem.
- Refactor code: Once the tests pass, developers can refactor the code to improve its design, readability, and maintainability. This includes removing duplicate code, renaming variables and methods, and improving the code structure.
- Run tests again: After refactoring the code, developers should run the tests again to ensure that the code still works as expected. If any tests fail, they should repeat steps 1-3 until all tests pass.

By following this process, developers can ensure that their code is well-tested, maintainable, and reliable. It also helps them catch errors early in the development process, reducing the time and cost of debugging and maintenance.

Advantages and disadvantages of TDD

Test-driven development (TDD) has several advantages and disadvantages, as outlined below:

Advantages:

- Improved code quality: TDD ensures that the code is thoroughly tested and meets the requirements of the client. This leads to a higher quality of the code.
- Faster development: TDD results in fewer defects, which means less time spent on bug fixing. This leads to faster development.
- Easier maintenance: As the code is thoroughly tested, it is easier to maintain and update in the future.
- Better communication: TDD encourages better communication between developers and clients. The client's requirements are defined and communicated through the tests.

Disadvantages:

- Time-consuming: Writing tests before writing code can be time-consuming and may increase the development time.
- Initial learning curve: TDD requires developers to learn new tools and techniques, which may take some time.
- Test maintenance: As the code changes, tests need to be updated as well. This can be a time-consuming process.
- May not catch all defects: While TDD reduces the number of defects, it may not catch all defects.

In summary, TDD has several advantages, including improved code quality, faster development, easier maintenance, and better communication. However, it also has some disadvantages, including being time-consuming, having an initial learning curve, test maintenance, and may not catch all defects.

Best practices for debugging and testing

Best practices for debugging and testing include:

- Use descriptive names for variables, methods, and classes to make the code easier to understand and debug.
- Use comments to explain the purpose of the code and how it works.
- Write small, focused test cases that target specific functionality.
- Use the AAA (Arrange, Act, Assert) pattern to structure your tests.
- Use an automated testing framework, such as NUnit, to run your tests automatically.
- Run your tests frequently during development to catch errors early.
- Use test doubles (mocks, stubs, etc.) to isolate code under test and make tests faster and more reliable.
- Use code coverage tools to ensure that your tests are covering all the important code paths.
- Use version control to manage your code and track changes.
- Follow the Single Responsibility Principle (SRP) to ensure that each class and method has a clear and well-defined purpose.
- Avoid writing complex code that is difficult to test.
- Use assertions to verify that the code behaves as expected.

By following these best practices, you can write better code, catch errors earlier, and create more reliable and maintainable software.

Writing effective test cases

Writing effective test cases is an important aspect of software testing. A test case is a set of steps or conditions under which a tester determines whether an application, software system, or one of its features functions properly. Effective test cases are important because they help ensure that software is reliable, efficient, and meets the requirements of its users. Here are some best practices for writing effective test cases:

- Clearly define the scope and purpose of the test case. This includes defining what is being tested, what the expected outcome is, and any preconditions or prerequisites required for the test.

- Use a consistent and organized format for test cases. This can include a header with the test case ID, a description of the test, the steps to execute the test, and the expected outcome.
- Make sure the test case is repeatable. This means that the test should produce the same results every time it is executed.
- Include both positive and negative test cases. Positive test cases verify that the software functions as expected when it is used as intended, while negative test cases verify that the software can handle unexpected or incorrect input.
- Consider boundary conditions and edge cases. These are conditions that are at the limits of what the software is designed to handle, and can be important for verifying the robustness of the software.
- Use test automation tools when appropriate. Test automation can help reduce the time and effort required for testing, and can also help ensure consistency and accuracy in testing.
- Regularly review and update test cases as necessary. This can help ensure that the test cases remain relevant and effective as the software evolves and changes over time.

In summary, writing effective test cases is an important aspect of software testing, and can help ensure that software is reliable, efficient, and meets the requirements of its users. Best practices for writing effective test cases include clearly defining the scope and purpose of the test case, using a consistent and organized format, making the test case repeatable, including both positive and negative test cases, considering boundary conditions and edge cases, using test automation tools when appropriate, and regularly reviewing and updating test cases as necessary.

Understanding code coverage and test coverage

Code coverage and test coverage are metrics that are used to measure the extent to which a software application has been tested. Code coverage measures the percentage of code that has been executed during testing, while test coverage measures the percentage of test cases that have been executed.

Code coverage can be measured using a code coverage tool that analyzes the code to determine which statements, branches, and paths have been executed during testing. The tool generates a report that shows the percentage of code that has been covered by the tests. Code coverage is a useful metric for identifying areas of the code that have not been tested and for measuring the effectiveness of the testing process.

Test coverage, on the other hand, measures the percentage of test cases that have been executed during testing. This metric is useful for identifying gaps in the test suite and for ensuring that all important scenarios have been covered. Test coverage can be measured using a test coverage tool that tracks the execution of each test case and generates a report that shows the percentage of test cases that have been executed.

While code coverage and test coverage are useful metrics for measuring the effectiveness of the testing process, they have some limitations. Code coverage only measures the extent to which code has been executed and does not take into account the quality of the tests. Test coverage only measures the extent to which test cases have been executed and does not take into account the quality of the code. Therefore, it is important to use these metrics in conjunction with other testing techniques, such as exploratory testing and code reviews, to ensure that the software application is thoroughly tested and meets the required quality standards.

Using test doubles (mocks, stubs, fakes) for isolated testing

Test doubles are objects or functions that are used in place of real dependencies during testing to isolate the unit being tested. The most commonly used types of test doubles are mocks, stubs, and fakes.

- Mocks are objects that mimic real objects and are used to verify inter-actions with them. They are useful when testing interactions between objects or components.
- Stubs are objects that return a pre-defined value or behavior and are used

to simulate specific conditions in the code being tested. They are useful when testing functions that depend on external factors or services.

- Fakes are objects that provide a simplified implementation of a real object or component. They are useful when testing complex or expensive objects or services.

Using test doubles is important for isolated testing because it allows you to test a specific unit of code without worrying about the behavior of its dependencies. This makes testing more reliable and easier to maintain. Additionally, using test doubles can help identify bugs or issues in your code before they cause problems in a production environment.

When using test doubles, it's important to ensure that they are properly configured and tested to accurately simulate the behavior of the real objects they are replacing. This can be achieved by using good naming conventions, writing clear and concise tests, and following best practices for testing and quality assurance.

Automating testing and continuous integration

Automating testing and continuous integration (CI) are important practices in modern software development. By automating tests and integrating them into the development process, teams can ensure that their code is working as expected, catch errors early on, and prevent regressions.

Automated testing involves running tests automatically using testing frameworks and tools, such as NUnit or MSTest in C#. These tests can be run locally or as part of a CI pipeline, where they are triggered automatically every time a change is made to the codebase.

Continuous integration is a practice of integrating code changes into a shared repository frequently and automatically, often multiple times a day. This is done to catch integration issues early on and ensure that the code is always in a releasable state. CI is typically achieved through the use of a build server, such as Jenkins or Travis CI, which automatically compiles, tests, and packages the code every time a change is made.

To get the most out of automated testing and CI, it's important to follow best practices such as writing effective test cases, using test doubles (mocks, stubs, fakes) for isolated testing, and ensuring good code coverage and test coverage. By following these practices, teams can build robust and reliable software with fewer bugs and faster release cycles.

10

Best Practices

Best practices in software development refer to the set of guidelines, prin-ciples, and recommended approaches that are widely accepted as the most effective and efficient ways of developing high-quality software. These prac-tices are based on years of experience and research by software development professionals and organizations and aim to ensure that software is reliable, maintainable, scalable, and meets the needs of its users.

Best practices cover various aspects of software development, including coding conventions, error handling and debugging, testing and quality assurance, performance optimization, and version control. By following these practices, developers can reduce the risk of errors, improve code quality, and increase the likelihood of successful project outcomes.

While best practices can vary depending on the programming language, platform, and development environment used, they generally share common principles and objectives. These include:

- Simplicity: Keeping code and processes as simple as possible to reduce the risk of errors and improve maintainability.
- Consistency: Applying consistent coding and design standards to ensure that code is easy to read and understand.
- Modularity: Breaking down code into smaller, more manageable modules that can be tested and maintained separately.

- Flexibility: Designing software with the ability to adapt to changing requirements and environments.
- Performance: Optimizing software for performance without sacrificing readability, maintainability, or scalability.
- Robustness: Ensuring that software can handle a range of inputs and scenarios, and recover gracefully from errors.

By adhering to these principles and other best practices, developers can produce software that is reliable, efficient, and effective, and meets the needs of its users.

Coding conventions

Coding conventions refer to a set of guidelines and best practices for writing code in a consistent and maintainable way. In C#, there are many coding conventions that developers can follow to improve the readability and maintainability of their code. Some of the most important coding conventions in C# include:

- Naming conventions: This includes guidelines for naming variables, methods, classes, and other program elements. For example, it is common to use PascalCase for class names and camelCase for method and variable names.
- Formatting conventions: This includes guidelines for formatting code, such as indentation, line breaks, and spacing. Consistent formatting can make code easier to read and understand.
- Commenting conventions: This includes guidelines for writing comments in code. Comments should be used sparingly, but when used, they should be clear and informative.
- Error handling conventions: This includes guidelines for handling errors and exceptions in code. Code should be written to handle errors gracefully and provide informative error messages to users.
- Code organization conventions: This includes guidelines for organizing

code into classes, methods, and other program elements. Code should be organized in a logical and easy-to-understand way.

Following coding conventions can make code easier to read, understand, and maintain. It can also make collaboration with other developers easier by providing a common set of guidelines to follow.

Choosing a coding style and adhering to it

Choosing a coding style and adhering to it is an important aspect of writing maintainable and readable code. A coding style defines a set of conventions for formatting and organizing code that help to ensure consistency across different code files and projects.

Some common coding style conventions include:

- Naming conventions for variables, functions, and classes
- Indentation and spacing
- Braces and parentheses placement
- Commenting style and documentation
- File organization and project structure

Choosing a coding style that fits your team's preferences and project require-ments can help to improve code readability and make it easier to maintain over time. Adhering to the chosen coding style consistently across all code files can also help to avoid confusion and errors when working with multiple developers.

Some tools and frameworks also provide built-in support for enforcing coding conventions, such as code analysis tools and linters. Using these tools can help to catch and fix coding style issues early in the development process.

Using descriptive and meaningful names for variables, classes, and methods

When writing code, it is important to use descriptive and meaningful names for variables, classes, and methods. This makes the code more readable and easier to understand for both the author and other developers who may work on the code later. Here are some best practices for naming conventions in C#:

- Use descriptive names: Names should accurately reflect the purpose and meaning of the variable, class, or method. Avoid using single-letter names or abbreviated names that are difficult to understand.
- Use PascalCase for class and method names: PascalCase is a naming convention where the first letter of each word is capitalized. This convention is commonly used for class and method names in C#.
- Use camelCase for variable names: camelCase is a naming convention where the first letter of the first word is lowercase and the first letter of each subsequent word is capitalized. This convention is commonly used for variable names in C#.
- Use meaningful prefixes for variable names: Adding a meaningful prefix to a variable name can help clarify its purpose. For example, using "is" as a prefix for a boolean variable that represents a true/false value can make its purpose clearer.
- Avoid using reserved words: C# has a set of reserved words that have a special meaning in the language. Avoid using these words as variable, class, or method names.

By following these best practices for naming conventions, you can make your code more readable and easier to understand, both for yourself and for other developers who may work on the code in the future.

Organizing code into logical and readable blocks

Organizing code into logical and readable blocks is an essential best practice in software development. Code organization makes it easier to understand, maintain, and modify code over time. Here are some tips for organizing code:

- Use meaningful names for classes, methods, and variables that accurately describe their purpose.
- Use comments to explain complex code or provide additional context.
- Group related code into functions or methods to make it easier to reuse and test.
- Use whitespace and indentation to visually separate code blocks and improve readability.
- Organize files and directories in a logical and consistent manner, such as grouping related files together or following a naming convention.

By organizing code in a logical and readable manner, developers can save time and reduce errors in the long run.

Error handling and debugging

Effective error handling and debugging are crucial for creating robust and maintainable software. Here are some best practices to follow:

- Use meaningful error messages: Error messages should provide helpful information that enables users to understand what went wrong and how to resolve the issue.
- Handle errors gracefully: Anticipate potential errors and handle them in a way that doesn't crash the program. For example, use try-catch blocks to catch exceptions and handle them appropriately.
- Log errors and exceptions: Logging errors and exceptions can help you identify and diagnose issues in production environments.
- Use the debugger: The debugger is a powerful tool that allows you to step

through your code and inspect variables and objects at runtime.

- Write automated tests: Automated tests can help catch errors early in the development process, reducing the likelihood of bugs in production.
- Follow the SOLID principles: SOLID is a set of principles that help you write code that is maintainable and easy to debug.
- Keep code simple and maintainable: Simplify your code to reduce the likelihood of errors and make it easier to debug when issues arise.

By following these best practices, you can create code that is more reliable, easier to maintain, and more resilient to errors and exceptions.

Handling errors gracefully

When developing software, it is important to anticipate and handle errors that may occur during the execution of the program. Handling errors gracefully means designing the code to respond appropriately to unexpected situations, such as invalid user input or system errors.

Here are some best practices for handling errors gracefully:

- Use try-catch blocks: Use try-catch blocks to catch and handle exceptions that may occur during program execution. This allows the program to gracefully recover from errors and continue running.
- Provide meaningful error messages: Provide descriptive error messages that help the user understand what went wrong and how to fix the problem.
- Validate input: Validate all user input to ensure that it is valid and within expected parameters. This can help prevent errors from occurring in the first place.
- Log errors: Log errors and exceptions that occur during program execution to help identify and diagnose problems. This can also help developers improve the code and prevent similar errors from occurring in the future.
- Use assertions: Use assertions to check for conditions that should never occur. This can help catch errors early and prevent them from causing

more serious problems down the line.

By following these best practices, developers can ensure that their programs handle errors gracefully and provide a better user experience.

Using exceptions for error handling

In C#, exceptions are a common way to handle errors that occur during program execution. Exceptions allow you to "throw" an error to indicate that something went wrong, and then "catch" that error to handle it in a specific way.

Using exceptions for error handling in C# involves several steps:

- Identifying potential error conditions in your code: This can include things like input validation, resource allocation, network connectivity, and more.
- Throwing an exception when an error occurs: This is done using the **throw** keyword, which creates an exception object and passes it up the call stack until it is caught by a matching **catch** block.
- Catching exceptions: To handle exceptions, you use a **try...catch** block. The **try** block contains the code that may throw an exception, while the **catch** block contains the code that handles the exception.
- Handling exceptions appropriately: Depending on the type of exception and the context of your code, you may choose to handle exceptions in different ways. This can include logging the error, displaying an error message to the user, or taking corrective action to address the error.

By using exceptions for error handling, you can make your code more robust and resilient to unexpected errors. However, it's important to use exceptions judiciously and to handle them appropriately to avoid creating more problems than you solve.

Debugging code effectively

Debugging code effectively involves identifying and fixing errors or bugs in the code. Here are some best practices for effective debugging:

- Use a debugger: Debuggers allow you to step through your code, line by line, to see where it is going wrong. They also allow you to inspect variables and objects to help you identify the source of the error.
- Reproduce the error: Before you start debugging, it is important to be able to reproduce the error consistently. This will help you narrow down the cause of the error and ensure that you have fixed it properly.
- Break down the problem: Debugging complex code can be overwhelming, so it is important to break down the problem into smaller, more manageable parts. Start by isolating the code that is causing the error and then work your way outwards from there.
- Check your assumptions: Often, errors occur because of incorrect assumptions about the state of the code or the values of variables. Double-check your assumptions to ensure that they are correct.
- Use print statements: If you are unable to use a debugger, adding print statements to your code can help you identify where the error is occurring. Print statements can be especially helpful when trying to isolate the source of the error.
- Test your fixes: Once you have identified and fixed the error, it is important to test your code thoroughly to ensure that the error has been resolved and that your fix has not introduced new errors.

In summary, effective debugging involves using a debugger, reproducing the error, breaking down the problem, checking your assumptions, using print statements, and testing your fixes. By following these best practices, you can identify and fix errors in your code quickly and efficiently.

Testing and quality assurance

Testing and quality assurance refer to the process of verifying that a software application meets its requirements, specifications, and standards. In the software development lifecycle, testing and quality assurance are crucial steps that ensure the reliability, functionality, and usability of a product.

Testing and quality assurance involve a range of activities, such as:

- Planning and designing test cases and scenarios based on requirements and user stories.
- Executing tests and recording results to identify defects, errors, and issues in the software.
- Debugging and fixing defects, errors, and issues.
- Tracking and managing defects, errors, and issues using a bug tracking system.
- Conducting different types of tests, such as unit tests, integration tests, system tests, acceptance tests, and regression tests.
- Ensuring compliance with coding standards, best practices, and industry standards.
- Performing code reviews and audits to identify potential issues and improve code quality.
- Using automated testing tools and frameworks to increase efficiency and coverage.

Effective testing and quality assurance can help to ensure that the software is reliable, robust, and performs as expected under different scenarios and conditions. This can result in higher customer satisfaction, fewer support calls, and lower maintenance costs.

Writing effective unit tests

Writing effective unit tests involves several best practices, including:

- Testing small units of code: Unit tests should focus on testing small, isolated units of code, such as individual methods or functions.
- Testing all possible cases: Unit tests should test all possible cases of the code being tested, including edge cases and boundary conditions.
- Testing for expected results: Unit tests should assert that the code being tested produces the expected results for each test case.
- Writing independent tests: Unit tests should be written to be independent of each other, so that the failure of one test does not affect the results of other tests.
- Using test data that is representative: Unit tests should use test data that is representative of the data that the code will encounter in real-world use.
- Testing early and often: Unit tests should be written early in the development process and run frequently to catch errors as early as possible.
- Keeping tests up-to-date: Unit tests should be kept up-to-date as the code changes to ensure that they continue to test the correct behavior of the code.

By following these best practices, developers can create effective unit tests that improve the quality and reliability of their code.

Analyzing code coverage and quality metrics

Analyzing code coverage and quality metrics is an essential part of software development to ensure the code is of high quality, maintainable, and meets the requirements. Analyzing code coverage and quality metrics involves the use of various tools and techniques to measure the quality of code and identify any potential issues that may impact the performance, scalability, or security of the software system.

Code coverage is the measure of the amount of code that has been tested by the test suite. It is an important metric to evaluate the effectiveness of the test suite and to identify any gaps in test coverage. Code coverage can be measured using tools such as dotCover, OpenCover, or NCover. These tools provide detailed reports on the code coverage of the test suite, including the lines of code executed, the percentage of code covered, and the number of tests executed.

Quality metrics are measurements used to assess the quality of software. These metrics can include measures of code complexity, maintainability, and testability. Common quality metrics include the cyclomatic complexity, the maintainability index, and the code smell detection. Tools such as ReSharper, SonarQube, and NDepend can be used to measure these metrics and provide detailed reports on the quality of the code.

Analyzing code coverage and quality metrics can help identify areas of the code that need improvement, such as improving test coverage or reducing code complexity. It can also help track the progress of the development process and ensure that the software is of high quality and meets the requirements.

In summary, analyzing code coverage and quality metrics is a critical aspect of software development to ensure the code is of high quality, maintainable, and meets the requirements. It involves measuring the amount of code covered by the test suite and assessing the quality of the code using various metrics. These tools and techniques help identify areas of the code that need improvement and ensure the software is of high quality and meets the requirements.

Version control with Git

Version control is a system that records changes to a file or set of files over time, so that you can recall specific versions later. Git is a popular distributed version control system that allows you to track changes to files over time, collaborate with others on a project, and revert to earlier versions if necessary.

Here are some of the key concepts and features of Git:

- Repository: A repository is a collection of files that you are tracking with Git. It contains all the files, folders, and subfolders for a project.
- Commit: A commit is a snapshot of your repository at a particular point in time. It records changes you've made to your files, such as adding, modifying, or deleting them.
- Branch: A branch is a separate line of development that allows you to work on new features or bug fixes without affecting the main branch.
- Merge: Merging is the process of combining two or more branches of development back into a single branch. This is typically done after changes have been made on separate branches and need to be integrated back into the main branch.
- Pull request: A pull request is a request to merge changes from one branch into another. This is typically done when you want to merge changes made by others into your own branch or when you want to merge your changes into another branch.
- Conflict: A conflict occurs when Git is unable to automatically merge two branches because they have made changes to the same lines of code. This can occur when two people are working on the same file and make different changes to the same line.

To use Git, you'll need to install it on your computer and then create a repository for your project. Once you have a repository, you can start making commits to record changes to your files. You can also create and switch between branches, merge changes from different branches, and use pull requests to collaborate with others.

Git also provides many other features and tools for working with repositories, including tags, remote repositories, and the ability to revert to earlier versions of your code. By using Git, you can easily track changes to your code over time, collaborate with others on a project, and ensure that your code is always up-to-date and free of errors.

Collaborating with others using Git

Collaborating with others using Git involves using Git to share and manage changes to a codebase between multiple developers. This process involves creating and managing branches, merging changes, and resolving conflicts. Here are some best practices for collaborating with others using Git:

- Use a shared repository: To collaborate on a project, all team members should work from a shared repository that acts as a central location for the codebase. This helps ensure that all changes are tracked and synced.
- Create and use feature branches: To work on a specific feature or bug fix, developers should create a new branch from the main branch. This allows multiple developers to work on different features simultaneously without interfering with each other's code.
- Review and merge changes: Once a developer has completed work on a feature branch, they should submit a pull request for code review. Code review ensures that the changes are in line with the project's goals and adheres to best practices. If the code is approved, it can be merged into the main branch.
- Resolve conflicts: When merging changes from multiple branches, conflicts can arise when two developers make changes to the same line of code. Conflicts need to be resolved before the changes can be merged. Git provides tools for resolving conflicts, but it requires careful attention to ensure that changes are not lost.
- Use descriptive commit messages: When committing changes to Git, it's important to use descriptive commit messages that explain what changes were made and why. This helps other developers understand the codebase's history and makes it easier to track down issues later on.

By following these best practices, teams can effectively collaborate using Git to manage changes to a codebase.

Using branching and merging effectively

Branching and merging are powerful features in Git that allow developers to work on different versions of code simultaneously and merge their changes together. Here's an overview of how to use branching and merging effectively in Git:

- Creating a branch: A branch is a separate version of the code that can be edited independently of the main codebase. To create a branch in Git, use the command "git branch branch_name". This will create a new branch with the given name.
- Switching to a branch: To switch to a different branch in Git, use the command "git checkout branch_name". This will switch to the specified branch and make it the active branch.
- Making changes on a branch: Once you're on a branch, you can make changes to the code as you normally would. These changes will only be applied to the branch you're currently on.
- Committing changes: After you've made changes on a branch, you'll need to commit those changes to save them to the Git repository. To do this, use the command "git commit -m 'Commit message'".
- Merging branches: When you're ready to merge changes from one branch into another, you'll need to use the "git merge" command. This will combine the changes from the specified branch into the active branch.
- Resolving conflicts: Sometimes, when you merge branches, there may be conflicts between the changes in the two branches. Git will prompt you to resolve these conflicts before the merge can be completed. This involves manually editing the affected files to resolve the conflicts.
- Deleting a branch: Once you're done with a branch, you can delete it using the command "git branch -d branch_name". This will delete the specified branch from the Git repository.

In summary, branching and merging are powerful features in Git that allow developers to work on different versions of code simultaneously and merge their changes together. By creating, switching between, and merging branches, developers can work more efficiently and avoid conflicts when making changes to a codebase.

11

Building Utilities

Building utilities is a common task in software development. A utility is a small, specialized program that performs a specific task, often in a command-line or console environment. Examples of utilities include file renaming tools, password generators, directory organizers, file deletion tools, duplicate file finders, and system information viewers.

Building utilities requires a good understanding of programming fundamentals, including data types, control structures, and functions. In addition, you will need to understand how to interact with the file system, read and write data to files, and parse command-line arguments.

You will also need to have a good understanding of the tools and technologies used in building utilities, such as regular expressions, data structures, and algorithms. Effective error handling and debugging skills are also essential.

In this book, we will explore the basics of building utilities using C#. We will cover a range of topics, from basic programming concepts to advanced techniques for working with the file system, regular expressions, and testing. We will also cover best practices for developing high-quality, maintainable code, and for collaborating effectively with others using version control tools like Git.

By the end of this book, you will have the skills and knowledge needed to build a wide range of powerful and useful utilities, and to contribute effectively to software development projects.

GetFileSize Utility

here's a basic outline for a file size finder utility:

1. Prompt the user for the path of the file they want to check.
2. Use the File class in the System.IO namespace to get information about the file, including its size.
3. Print the file size to the console in a human-readable format (e.g. "File size: 2.5 MB").
4. Give the user the option to check the size of another file or exit the program.

Here's some sample code that implements this functionality:

```
 4    using System;
 5    using System.IO;
 6
 7    namespace FileSizeFinder
 8    {
 9        class Program
10        {
11            static void Main(string[] args)
12            {
13                while (true)
14                {
15                    Console.Write("Enter path of file to check (type 'exit' to quit): ");
16                    string filePath = Console.ReadLine();
17
18                    if (filePath.ToLower() == "exit")
19                        break;
20
21                    try
22                    {
23                        FileInfo fileInfo = new FileInfo(filePath);
24
25                        if (fileInfo.Exists)
26                        {
27                            double fileSizeMB = (double)fileInfo.Length / (1024 * 1024);
28                            Console.WriteLine($"File size: {fileSizeMB:N2} MB");
29                        }
30                        else
31                        {
32                            Console.WriteLine("File not found.");
33                        }
34                    }
35                    catch (Exception ex)
36                    {
37                        Console.WriteLine($"Error: {ex.Message}");
38                    }
39
40                    Console.WriteLine();
41                }
42            }
43        }
44    }
```

Note that this is just a simple implementation, and there are many ways you could expand or modify this utility depending on your specific needs.

The source code for this utility can be downloaded at https://github.com/m topsolutions/FileSizeFinder/releases/tag/v1.0.0.0

GetSystemInfo Utility

Create the SystemInfo Class

```
48    using System;
49    using System.Collections.Generic;
50    using System.Linq;
51    using System.Text;
52    using System.Threading.Tasks;
53
54    namespace SystemInfo
55    {
56        public static class SystemInfo
57        {
58            public static void GetSystemInfo()
59            {
60                Console.WriteLine("==== SYSTEM INFORMATION ====");
61                Console.WriteLine($"OS Version: {Environment.OSVersion}");
62                Console.WriteLine($"64-bit OS: {Environment.Is64BitOperatingSystem}");
63                Console.WriteLine($"Machine Name: {Environment.MachineName}");
64                Console.WriteLine($"Processor Count: {Environment.ProcessorCount}");
65                Console.WriteLine($"System Directory: {Environment.SystemDirectory}");
66                Console.WriteLine($"User Name: {Environment.UserName}");
67                Console.WriteLine($"User Domain Name: {Environment.UserDomainName}");
68                Console.WriteLine($"Working Set: {Environment.WorkingSet}");
69                Console.WriteLine($"CLR Version: {Environment.Version}");
70                Console.WriteLine("=================================");
71            }
72        }
73    }
```

To use the SystemInfo class, follow these steps:

1. Create a new console application in Visual Studio or any other IDE.
2. Add a reference to the SystemInfo namespace in your code file.
3. Call the GetSystemInfo method of the SystemInfo class from your Main method.
4. Build and run your console application.

Here's an example usage of the SystemInfo in a console application:

```
77
78    using SystemInfo;
79    using System;
80
81
82    class Program
83    {
84        static void Main(string[] args)
85        {
86            SystemInfo.SystemInfo.GetSystemInfo();
87            Console.ReadKey();
88        }
89    }
```

This will display the system information on the console when the program is run.

The source code for this utility can be downloaded at https://github.com/m topsolutions/FileCopyUtility/releases/tag/v1.0.0.0

FileCopyUtility

Here is an example console application in C# that copies a file and renames it:

```
93    using System;
94    using System.IO;
95
96    namespace FileCopyUtility
97    {
98        class Program
99        {
100           static void Main(string[] args)
101           {
102               if (args.Length != 2)
103               {
104                   Console.WriteLine("Usage: FileCopyUtility
105                           <source file> <destination file>");
106                   return;
107               }
108
109               string sourceFile = args[0];
110               string destinationFile = args[1];
111
112               try
113               {
114                   File.Copy(sourceFile, destinationFile);
115                   Console.WriteLine($"Successfully copied '{sourceFile}'
116                           to '{destinationFile}'");
117
118                   string newFileName = Path.GetFileNameWithoutExtension(destinationFile)
119                           + "_copy" + Path.GetExtension(destinationFile);
120                   string newFilePath = Path.Combine(Path.GetDirectoryName
121                           (destinationFile), newFileName);
122                   File.Move(destinationFile, newFilePath);
123
124                   Console.WriteLine($"Renamed copied file to '{newFileName}'");
125               }
126               catch (Exception ex)
127               {
128                   Console.WriteLine($"Error copying file: {ex.Message}");
129               }
130           }
131       }
132   }
```

To use this utility, you can run the executable from the command line and pass in the source file and destination file paths as arguments, like this:

```
135
136   FileCopyUtility.exe C:\path\to\source\file.txt D:\path\to\destination\file.txt
137
```

This will copy the source file to the destination file path, and then rename the copied file to include "_copy" in the file name.

The source code for this utility can be downloaded at https://github.com/m topsolutions/GetSystemInfo/releases/tag/V1.0.0.0

CreateDirectories Utility

Here's an example console application in C# that reads a list of directories from a CSV file and creates those directories if they don't already exist:

```
139    System;
140    System.IO;
141    System.Linq;
142
143    ace CreateDirectoriesFromCSV
144
145    ass Program
146
147      static void Main(string[] args)
148      {
149          // Get the path to the CSV file from the command line arguments
150          if (args.Length < 1)
151          {
152              Console.WriteLine("Usage:
153                  CreateDirectoriesFromCSV <csv file>");
154              return;
155          }
156          string csvFilePath = args[0];
157
158          // Read the list of directories from the CSV file
159          string[] directories = File.ReadLines(csvFilePath)
160                              .Where(line =>
161                              !string.IsNullOrWhiteSpace(line))
162                              .ToArray();
163
164          // Create each directory if it doesn't already exist
165          foreach (string directory in directories)
166          {
167              if (!Directory.Exists(directory))
168              {
169                  try
170                  {
171                      Directory.CreateDirectory(directory);
172                      Console.WriteLine($"Created directory: {directory}");
173                  }
174                  catch (Exception ex)
175                  {
176                      Console.WriteLine($"Failed to create
177                          directory {directory}: {ex.Message}");
178                  }
179              }
180          }
181      }
182
```

To use this utility, you need to create a CSV file containing the list of directories you want to create, with one directory per line. Then you can run the utility from the command line like this:

```
184    CreateDirectoriesFromCSV.exe <csv file>
185
```

Replace **<csv file>** with the path to the CSV file you created. The utility will read the list of directories from the CSV file and create each directory if it doesn't already exist.

The source code for this utility can be downloaded at https://github.com/m topsolutions/CreateDirectories/releases/tag/v1.0.0.0

Glossary

1. Abstract Class - A class that cannot be instantiated and can only be used as a base class for other classes. It contains at least one abstract method and may contain concrete methods as well.
2. Access Modifier - A keyword that determines the level of access to a class, method, or variable from other parts of the code. Examples include public, private, protected, and internal.
3. Asynchronous Programming - A programming model that allows multiple operations to be performed simultaneously, without blocking the main thread of execution. It relies on tasks, which are units of work that can be executed concurrently.
4. Base Class - A class from which other classes are derived. It provides the common properties and methods that are inherited by its derived classes.
5. Collection - An object that contains a group of elements or objects. Examples include arrays, lists, dictionaries, and sets.
6. Constructor - A special method that is called when an object of a class is created. It initializes the object's data members and sets its initial state.
7. C# - A modern, object-oriented programming language developed by Microsoft. It is widely used for developing desktop applications, web applications, and games.
8. Debugging - The process of finding and fixing errors or bugs in a program. It involves tools and techniques that help identify and isolate problems in the code.
9. Delegation - A programming pattern where an object passes responsibility for a task to another object. It is achieved using delegates, which

are objects that encapsulate a method and can be passed as arguments to other methods.

10. Encapsulation – A principle of object-oriented programming that restricts direct access to an object's data members and exposes them through methods. It helps maintain data integrity and provides a clear interface for interacting with objects.

11. Enum – A value type that represents a set of named constants. It can be used to define a group of related values that have a common purpose.

12. Exception – An object that represents an error condition or unexpected situation that occurs during the execution of a program. It can be caught and handled using try-catch blocks.

13. Generic – A type that can be parameterized with one or more type arguments. It allows for greater flexibility and code reuse in a program.

14. IDE – An integrated development environment that provides tools and features for coding, debugging, and testing software. Examples include Visual Studio and JetBrains Rider.

15. Inheritance – A mechanism in object-oriented programming where one class (the derived class) inherits the properties and methods of another class (the base class).

16. Interface – A contract that defines a set of methods and properties that a class must implement. It allows for polymorphism and separation of concerns in a program.

17. LINQ – Language Integrated Query. A set of language features in C# that allow for querying data sources such as collections and databases using a uniform syntax. It provides a powerful and concise way to work with data.

18. Namespace – A container that holds a group of related classes, structures, and other types. It provides a way to organize and group related code in a program.

19. Nullable – A type that can contain either a value or null. It is useful for representing optional or missing values in a program.

20. Object – The base class for all types in C#. It provides common methods such as ToString() and Equals().

21. Operator - A symbol or keyword that performs a specific operation on one or more operands. Examples include +, -, *, /, and ==.

22. Overloading - A feature of C# that allows multiple methods or operators to have the same name but different parameter lists. It provides a way to provide different behaviors for related operations.

23. Inheritance - Inheritance is the process of creating a new class from an existing class. The new class is known as the derived class, and the existing class is known as the base class. The derived class inherits all the properties, methods, and fields of the base class. It also adds its own unique properties, methods, and fields.

24. Interface - An interface is a set of methods, properties, and events that define a contract. Any class that implements an interface must implement all the members of the interface. An interface defines the behavior of a class without specifying how that behavior is implemented.

25. Lambda Expression - A lambda expression is a concise way of representing a delegate method. It is an anonymous function that can be used to create delegates or expression tree types. Lambda expressions provide a compact and easy-to-read way of writing code that performs simple operations.

26. LINQ - LINQ (Language Integrated Query) is a set of extensions to the C# language that allows you to query data from different data sources using a unified syntax. It provides a standard query syntax for querying data from different data sources such as databases, XML documents, and in-memory data structures.

27. Namespace - A namespace is a collection of related classes, structures, interfaces, and other types. It provides a way to organize code and avoid naming conflicts. Namespaces also enable you to use code from other libraries without having to fully qualify the names of the types.

28. Null Coalescing Operator - The null coalescing operator (??) is used to provide a default value when a nullable value is null. It returns the left-hand operand if it is not null, otherwise it returns the right-hand operand.

29. Object Initializer - An object initializer is a way of creating an instance

of a class and setting its properties in a single expression. It provides a concise and readable way of initializing objects.

30. Operator Overloading – Operator overloading is a technique that allows operators to be redefined for user-defined types. It enables you to define how operators such as +, -, *, /, and % are used with your own custom types.

31. Partial Class – A partial class is a class that is split into multiple files. Each file contains a separate part of the class, but they are all combined to form a single class when the code is compiled. Partial classes are useful for breaking up large classes into smaller, more manageable parts.

32. Polymorphism – Polymorphism is the ability of an object to take on many forms. In C#, polymorphism is achieved through inheritance and interfaces. A derived class can be treated as its base class or as an instance of its own type. An interface can be implemented by any class, enabling polymorphic behavior.

33. Property – A property is a member of a class that provides a way to access and set the value of a private field. It is a combination of a getter method and a setter method, which are used to get and set the value of the property.

34. Reflection – Reflection is a set of APIs that allows you to inspect and interact with metadata, types, and objects at runtime. It provides a way to discover information about a type and its members, and to dynamically create instances of a type, invoke its methods, and access its properties.

35. Struct – A struct is a value type that is similar to a class, but with some important differences. It is a lightweight alternative to a class that is commonly used to represent simple data structures. Unlike classes, structs are value types and are allocated on the stack rather than the heap.

36. Namespace: A namespace is a container for a group of related types that can be used to organize your code and prevent naming conflicts.

37. Object: An instance of a class is called an object. It is a self-contained entity that contains data and the code to manipulate the data.

38. Operator: An operator is a symbol that represents an action to be

performed on one or more operands.

39. Polymorphism: Polymorphism is the ability of an object to take on many forms. In C#, polymorphism is achieved through inheritance and interfaces.

40. Property: A property is a member that provides a flexible mechanism to read, write, or compute the value of a private field.

41. Reflection: Reflection is a feature in C# that allows you to inspect and manipulate metadata at runtime.

42. Regular Expression: A regular expression is a pattern used to match text strings. C# has a built-in regular expression engine that allows you to use regular expressions to search, replace, and validate text.

43. Static: The static keyword is used to declare a member that belongs to the type itself instead of a specific instance of the type.

44. Struct: A struct is a value type that can contain data members and methods. It is similar to a class but has some differences in behavior and performance.

45. Task: A Task is an object that represents an asynchronous operation in C#. It allows you to perform operations in the background while still allowing the user to interact with the application.

46. Type: A type is a classification of data that specifies the set of values and operations that can be performed on those values.

47. Using: The using statement is used to declare a scope in which one or more resources can be used and then disposed of automatically when the scope is exited.

48. Variable: A variable is a named storage location in memory that can hold a value of a specific type.

49. Virtual: The virtual keyword is used to declare a method, property, or event that can be overridden by a derived class.

50. Yield: The yield keyword is used to create an iterator in C#. It allows you to return a sequence of values one at a time, which can be more efficient than returning an entire collection at once.